To Alan

Rethreading my Life

Alanna McIntyre

continue with
your novel
I really like
it best wishes
Alanna 2014

Rethreading my Life is a personal memoir. Alanna McIntyre asserts the moral right to be identified as the author of this work.

ISBN 978-1-291-95096-0

A *NightWriters Editions* book

NightWriters Editions have been inaugurated in order to focus attention on individual writers living in or near Brighton whose work merits publication.

NightWriters Editions are published by NightWriters Press.
www.nightwriters.org.uk

Acknowledgements

This book is dedicated to Andy with love. It is a thank-you to my children Gemma and Justinian who have supported me throughout and to Kaia, my grandchild.

It is written for all my friends and others who have experienced loss in many forms, and to celebrate how living creatively allows healing to evolve. I acknowledge and appreciate how Jane Leclercq my EFT counsellor gave me the skills to come to terms with my loss.

My thanks to Tony Dugdale, Nigel Wrench, Vanessa Jones, Barbara Aston and Araminta Hall who have given their time and expertise, providing constructive criticism and helping me edit Rethreading my Life. My thanks and appreciation to Tim Shelton-Jones for his encouragement in my creative writing and his patience in copy editing the piece. I am grateful to Brighton NightWriters for their support. Joe Evans kindly designed the cover taking numerous pictures of my artwork on a glorious sunny day in my garden and producing an amazing result.

I also appreciate the support of Dawn Austin-Locke from Saltdean Library and Nicky Hayden from Upstairs at the Three and Ten in Brighton and Jo Merriman who gave their time and expertise to enable extracts of Rethreading my Life to be previewed in a dramatized form.

I also acknowledge the Whitehawk Inn, Community Centre of Learning, which has been a pivotal focus for me and I would like any profits from the sale of this book to go to the Whitehawk Inn **www.whinn.org.uk**.

FOREWORD

I have collated extracts from a sporadic diary since I separated from you in late 2008, and when you took your own life, probably on 16th December 2009. Your official date of death on the certificate is 2nd January 2010. This was the day you were found in a rented holiday flat by a cleaner. You were 56.

This diary-based book tells of your suicide, but also of the death of Pop, my Father, on 5th July 2011 at the age of 94.

I use driftwood finds. Sea twine is often interwoven with shells and driftwood, forming natural sculptures. Broken pieces can be made whole again.

My ritual morning exercise routine from emotional freedom therapy, qigong and yoga allow me to be focused in the present.

I have also assumed another role in life as an active granny looking after my granddaughter and supporting my daughter. This, together with my art, writing, working with clay, doing the garden, having massage therapy and healing, have provided me with a skeletal outline for my life.

The garden grounds me. The sea and water heal me and encourage my creative flow. I learn to let go and accept that sporadic memories of you

1

will float into my mind. Grief is a fractured bowl and within its fragments lies a reminder of wholeness.

I change. I love you from a distance. Friends that supported both of us are still there for me. I'm gradually seeking out new acquaintances, who may become friends. I'm learning to reshape and rethread my life.

Notes on Therapies

Emotional Freedom Therapy (EFT) involves tapping, together with using affirmations. It has over time become an instinctual habit which can help me when I am anxious and need to focus.

Qigong is a Chinese skill which helps me to become grounded and balanced and fine-tunes the mind in slow and deliberate movements.

Yoga helps me to be aware and in the present and allows me to realise the importance of my breath and my space. It also teaches me relaxation.

CHAPTER ONE

I need to make sense of separation and death. I make a start.

COURAGE AND LIGHT

"Light, love and courage," says a friend as I begin rethreading my life.

Initially you and I were separated by distance. You spent most of your last year in a mental health centre. We visited each other from time to time. Towards the end visits became less frequent as there was a need to disassociate from a relationship that was still caring but would not be able to work if we got together again.

I often find bus journeys a good place to scribble my thoughts down. One extract on the bus to Eastbourne, where you spent most of your life, apart from with me, was:-

The sun shines through the clouds into the sea, and I think of you. It makes the sea glisten, thoughts flicker like rays and the sea wells in tears.

My solar plexus, "What's that?" I hear you say, my gut churns, scrapes, whirls, and twirls in a cleansing action. The bus is moving very slowly, but steadily forward. Sometimes it stops, but doesn't move back, and is gently proceeding on its journey.

There are many roads to choose. Twenty five years our lives were spent together, now they each take a different route, as we see changing horizons. The love will not dissipate but evolve into self-loving and healing.

> You find endings very difficult
> You have had numerous attempts
> This is not an ending but a
> Different way of being,
> Where you gain self esteem
> Do not feel pressurised and
> Do your own thing.
> There is a great sadness
> In parting, each can find a
> Way without anger and
> Frustration, stillness in our
> Hearts, still respecting
> Each other for who we are.

My feelings are like dandelions whose shoots I pick, but never really dig down to pull up the root, that stains. Occasionally in the early morning tears pour down my face, until qigong has staunched my uprootedness. I move beyond welled grief to find solace and be open to the unexpected beach find, a smile, and a day out sitting in a divine garden supping summer tea. My grandchild helps me water the garden, nurturing my soul; there is joy. Even though separation splinters glass, the ebb and flow will smooth the sharp edges.

It is a day in December when your moods fluctuate like a darting dragonfly that is the turning point.

You went off to buy some milk and bread just after lunch. I was in our rented house waiting for your return. My stomach fluttered, I breathed deeply. I diverted myself by finding something trivial to occupy my mind. I was denying the fact that something could be wrong. Once it became dark I began to panic. I hoped you would come back like all the other times.

You had never spent a night away from home. I rang the library, somewhere you often sought refuge. I rang a friend I had made locally who had given you a massage. She said I should ring my children and the police. I was reluctant to do this. I had always coped on my own.

It felt like admitting defeat. I was no longer under control. I did phone the police and explained why I was worried because you had uncontrolled epilepsy and were also probably confused. I also contacted my children.

6

I was in the house alone when the police came and I answered their questions as far as I was able. They then searched the house and the large gardens in case you were hiding on the premises. It was only after their inspection that I realised you had taken some of your medication. The house was surrounded by a high fence. I realised the car had disappeared too.

You had not driven since we had met over 25 years before, as you realised the safety implications of your uncontrolled epilepsy. You had always wanted to drive again but were scared of hurting or killing yourself or other people. I was really shocked. It was out of character.

For the police, I had made a list of people you might have contacted or places you might try to visit. My daughter came with her young baby. Later that evening, nearer midnight, she went to collect my son from the station. We watched DVDs and then eventually snatched some sleep. My daughter was up early in the morning as she had work. She also did not want you to come back in a psychotic state with a vulnerable child in the house. She had already made arrangements for her daughter's care.

She came earlier in the year when you were rushed to hospital after you had swallowed bathroom cleaner 'Astonish', which contains bleach. You were discharged after a few hours. At the time of her visit you were sitting on the sofa and finding it difficult to swallow. Your eyes were glazed and you were sleepy. Initially when you awoke you were glad you were alive and cuddled me and said everything would be ok.

This time you had disappeared. The following morning I began to feel a prisoner in the house and needed some fresh air. Sometimes you said I made you feel a prisoner too.

My son was there to answer the phone. I felt free to go for a walk in the town.

I went to the bank. When I got to the counter I burst into tears. The staff knew both of us and ushered me into a small backroom. They gave me a cup of tea and checked your bank account to see if any money had been withdrawn. No money had been removed since your disappearance.

I left the bank and my mobile rang. It was my son to say you had rung your friends and were in an ambulance on the way to hospital. I ran back to the house. I rang the friends you'd spoken to who asked me if there was something wrong as you had been shouting, "I want a divorce!"

The hospital said you had taken an overdose of antidepressants and then, when they began to have an effect, you had panicked and rung them from a phone box.

My son and I went to the hospital. You were on a trolley sitting up and looking sweaty, pale and extremely unwell. Luckily you chose the hospital where they had your neurological notes.

My son and I were both in a state of shock. You said, "I'm sorry, I didn't mean it." A few minutes later you had a tonic-clonic seizure and as the trolley had bars I was afraid you might hurt yourself as your body convulsed strongly.

The team came to take over, and my son and I sat on the bench opposite the recovery room. You were taken in there and an airway was put down your throat and numerous blood tests and urine tests were taken. You were constantly monitored. The risk was that the medication you took could change your blood pressure, going from excessively low to very high, which could result in heart failure. They packed you with ice as you were very hot.

The doctor apologised for not being a neurologist and told us what medications he had used to try to stabilise your condition. He asked my advice on what he should try next. I suggested a drug to which he agreed.

He promised both of us you would not be transferred until your condition was stabilised. My son and I managed to get the last train back and then a taxi to the house.

We were both exhausted. The next morning we made the journey again. You had been transferred to the acute medical ward. The woman next to you had the curtains drawn round her bed and was in a very poorly state. I poured you some water and you drank it with very shaky hands. You could not remember where you had left the car, but could recall where you had stayed the night in a bed-and-breakfast.

We explained to a psychiatrist that there had been previous psychotic episodes, and also several suicide attempts. We also mentioned your uncontrolled epilepsy, obsessive compulsive behaviour, and personality disorder. She promised she would see you on the ward and assess how you were functioning.

To the outside world you could be normal; underneath, I could recognise the signs that you were not well. You were confused.

I had known you for twenty five years.

CHAPTER TWO

How much more can I stand? The pressure is building up – just like you before one of your seizures.

We returned home and the psychiatrist said that she had faxed the crisis team and you would be discharged to them. On the day of the discharge I found out that the faxed papers did not enable the crisis team to take over. The only support I would have would be dialling 999.

The single road to the hospital was 10 miles. I told the crisis team there was no way I could have you home without any back up. The crisis team had previously helped after the swallowed bathroom cleaner incident.

This was the first time I was given a carer's assessment. I had looked after you for more than twenty five years. The team sometimes ignored my crying on the end of the phone. They told me I was coping really well.

On the previous suicide attempt the neurologist thought you would be better at home. The support worker disagreed with him, but as the neurologist was the boss it was decided you stay at home with me with local help. The support worker comforted me when I cried with rage, sorrow and frustration.

11

This time something snapped. The fabric was torn. I told the crisis team it was impossible for me to cope under these circumstances. I could not have you back. It was totally unrealistic for you to live in our temporary home on your own without supervision. The owners who had allowed us to rent the house did not want another attempted suicide on their premises. The team would have to find a suitable place for you to go, as now you were homeless.

Immediately after your suicide attempts you were full of euphoria when you realised you were still alive. Then almost imperceptibly and insidiously, paranoia and confusion would take hold of you. This could last days or weeks. You would be in an altered state and often said you felt as though you had died.

The day of your arranged discharge started badly. Rain was followed by lightning and thunder. The electricity at our rented home went off and on spasmodically.

The children decided I should not stay in the house. I was crying uncontrollably, a mixture of relief and sadness. They became my parents. They supervised me packing my stuff and bundled me in the car, assuring me everything would be sorted. I went home to my Dad or Pop as we call him.

I knew if I'd stayed, you and I would both have sunk beneath the surface. I could no longer haul us into equilibrium. I cried for all the times there had been normality. There were times when fear dissipated and we could function together. Then terror would seize you. You did not trust me; you wanted to prove you could live independently.

I had learned to disassociate myself from the workings of your mind. I could only anchor myself. I saw facets of you which others didn't, and put up with ones I shouldn't. You wanted peace. You sometimes had this with me. Towards the end you felt the extremes of hate and love towards yourself.

I would have liked the medical profession to understand you. You were a complex man who needed help. They did not have the interventions, or the strategies. How do you cope with someone who sabotages a plan of action because their fear overrides them? Change is petrifying. Your brain needed rewiring.

The prescribed drugs for epilepsy may or may not have helped. They never really controlled your epilepsy and seizures punctuated your life. Sometimes the suppression of the seizures seemed to have worse side-effects than the seizures themselves. The brain can get used to having seizures, leading to them happening more frequently.

They left physical scars that healed, but the extent to which it damaged your brain is unknown.

When your mind was seized it would take you on tortuous trips where every word I said took on layers of meaning, reasoning gone. Fear unwrapped implied threats in an innocent phrase. I would pray for a seizure to stop this compulsive never-ending thought process. I would ask for stillness to calm an overactive imagination.

Pop had a spare room and I unpacked my stuff. This was only going to be a temporary solution.

My son and I eventually found out where the car was parked. The windscreen was covered with penalty notices but you had put an initial pay-and-display sticker on the car. You had left the door slightly ajar which meant the internal light had been on. The battery was dead. The contents of the glove compartment were intact. The scrap of paper with the emergency call out number was there. It was freezing and getting dark but the rescue services came as promised.

I managed the journey home but when nearly there I clipped a kerb. My concentration went just for a second.

During the initial crisis I found MIND and SANELINE invaluable for support and advice and saw a psychotherapist, who mirrored and repeated my feelings to me. She encouraged my writing and art, which are therapeutic.

I managed to build up a routine to my day, which I think was important to my survival. I then progressed from psychotherapy to Emotional Freedom Technique, which has suited me better in the long term. I have incorporated this into my daily life.

This crisis happened near Christmas and I felt guilty that you were in a mental institution, so I sent our joint cards to you and a present. My son and I visited you and bought the papers and things you needed. You were very contrite and went on bended knees, but I said that the only way forward was for us to have our own lives and find our own way. I would always be friends but could no longer live with you. I made sure that our friends knew of your mobile details and the particulars of the mental health centre. All our friends were mutually supportive.

This is the thank you that I wrote to my psychotherapist who encouraged my art and writing:-

> Thank you for being
> The listening face, mirroring
> My feelings. There will
> Be difficult days ahead
> Sadness and
> Unexpected joy
> Will be held together in waves
> Woven threads and words

Caught on the page.

I am moving to a different phase

Where the seed of love is shared

With many and into a place where

I can lay down roots.

You are now separate from me

Seeking a new path

A new way of living.

CHAPTER THREE

I need a place of my own, where I can be me.

I am seeing an EFT (Emotional Freedom Technique) counsellor and learning the technique of tapping. Initially the counsellor would put my fears and concerns into words and tap various parts of my body. I evolved my own affirmations and what I wanted to change in my life and how I wanted to feel. This is now part of my routine and not only do I tap for myself but others too. I sent you these lines:-

Be gentle on yourself
Enjoy the simple things
Let your love
Open your heart
Allow your breath to calm
Begin to feel grounded
In your own time and space
Let the inner peace
Surround you with warmth
Allow yourself to uncurl
Unwrap the love within.
Be grateful for simple things
A clear sky
A stranger's smile

A seagull perched
Or gliding on the thermal air
Calmness in your breath
Take care.

*When I was at Pop's and at a friend's house, I was naturally grateful
for somewhere to stay; but I did not find them to be places where I
could release my emotion. Often I would find myself crying in public
spaces like in a bus, whilst shopping or in the confines of my car. Tears
are a natural release and help the grieving process. I had moved from
Pop's into a short term bedsit. I wrote :-*

I cry in the shower
Missing you
Knowing we are separate.
We will survive.
Your repeatedly saying
"I don't want to hurt you"
Rings in my ears
When I phone you are calm
The warm shower comforts
My tears merge unseen with
Cleansing water, a busy
Day lies ahead,
Twenty five years have come to an end.

Sitting in a bedsit
Looking out at roof tops
Against the grey sky
Food is to be shared
To eat alone is difficult
Food is love prepared
It's giving. Bought three
Plants tête-a-tête, pale primula
With egg-yolk centre
And a blue hyacinth, now sit
On the window sill
Tendrils of growing hope.
I sit there crying
Missing your hand
In mine cuddling me
We see the same sky
But differently
It's hard so hard and
It's because my love is so strong
So I have to be stronger than
I sometimes feel I can be.
Time will smudge the rawness
And like scars will fade
And our caring for each other
Will show by looking

After ourselves.

Twenty five years fractured

Is part but not the whole.

We seek to find completeness

Without blame or hurt

Change is difficult

A new way for you and

A different way for me.

I was trying to accept that when you weren't well I was not able to improve your circumstances. Coming to terms with the feelings I had when dealing with things you always did.

The rage has disappeared

I can see you and not

Feel anguish or hurt.

I feel calm not threatened

By being separate and having

Times together. The love

Has re-emerged like the

Broken shard smoothed

By the erosion of the waves

And become a treasured

Fragment of glass

No longer broken

Made whole although
You feel numb
You too will find a
New life of your own.

I got upset when I realised by talking to you on the phone that you weren't well. I realised by the tone of your voice and the words you used. It was like reading sounds. A smile through clenched teeth outwardly expresses a grin, but inwardly something totally different.

I had still not disassociated myself from the role of carer. In the background I kept friends informed. I found out possible ways you could manage your new situation, and sent you details. I sent a long letter to your psychiatrist and Community Psychiatric Nurse outlining your problems.

As you always did all the financial stuff, I found dealing with this would make me feel angry, frustrated, sad and overwhelmed. Gradually I learned to cope with it step by step and tap when I needed to deal with something complicated. Sometimes the files are a bit messy but they will get tidied.

Every day is different. I can still not look at your handwriting. It's like holding your hand and letting it go.

We had enjoyable times when visiting friends but in the end you said coming back was a retrograde step. You still love me, but are afraid of doing things wrong. There are improvements but you are still agitated and nervous and your sleep is not good. I occasionally went to visit you and we looked at possible places for you to live.

I wrote this for my Emotional Freedom Counsellor:-

> You tap my face
> Tears choked
> My stomach feels raw
> I'm being pulled apart.
> You are empathetic and intuitive.
> You allow me to
> Cry in a safe and protected space.
> Your rhythm and tempo
> Are firm and assured and
> I feel I can be myself and
> Am accepted for who I am.
> There are no judgments
> Just the two of us.
> No space for criticism, I can ask questions
> So can you. I am naked and safe
> Surrounded by loving care and
> Ending with a breath for

Calmness and peace
And then a refreshing drink of water.

CHAPTER FOUR

With the help of my Emotional Freedom Technique I was able to come to terms with the fact that my relationship with you had affected my children. I also knew I loved you very much but needed to distance that love in a caring way.

Today I am able to admit that the hurt you caused my children could only be resolved by your death. I loved you and I still love you at a distance, but I sometimes put your needs before those of my children. You were not able to love them in the way I could and they felt rejected by you, like you felt excluded by society. You knew I missed being an active Granny and now I am that again. I gave you all that I could and you appreciated that.

Now I have my freedom to do as I please and so gradually the rift will heal. There is no blame. I loved you and my children. That never stopped. They are aware of that. I can love them openly.

I light the candle in your burner and the wooden duck and baby duck are on one side of it. The wooden bird with a springy neck is on the other side with the African metal blackbird that I bought in Chichester with you. The burner flickers. We are together but separate.

You loved me but caused me pain as well as joy over the twenty five years we were together. I gave you some kind of protection. You said I should have made you independent, but in the end you could not cope with life, either with me or alone. In the flame your light, like a star, flickers. The shape altering like the fire allowing us to be warmed but not harmed and I can love you from afar.

I choose to remember the good times and in the last year of separation there were no times of hate. I had learned to be strong, you had learned to let go.

I did, and I do, want others to be able to help people like you, and to understand.

I have been looking at the hazel twig in my sitting room and the felted heart with a heart-shaped hole, the other three hearts intact. The crystal catches the rainbow spectrum. Tears are gentle and cascade.

Both orchids are now again in bloom and the potted seeds and bulbs watered. The garden has pockets of colour. Like your blue silk hanky on our wedding day.

My grief is a little like the back door: sometimes it sticks and is a pain to open, other times when the weather is fine it's ok.

Today I transplanted some forget-me-nots that a friend had left on my doorstep. I put them by the chalk pieces I gather at the seaside and shells from here and abroad.

I try and see the flame in your burner from my workroom window. I cannot see the flame at first and then I see it flicker.

Your brain after a seizure would be on automatic pilot. You would be able to answer questions, but I knew you were not really conscious. It was only later you would be able to understand you had suffered a seizure. You would then recall a momentary foreboding just prior to the seizure, the last thing you saw, and then blank until the moment of realisation.

Yesterday I slept better. My grandchild was good company until she had a couple of strops. The fury, rage and tears were similar to your frustration. The anger stopped.

Had I protected you too much? I have learned to care for myself. You said I was a survivor. I am reworking my life.

I focus on what I need to do in my life and encourage change through positive affirmations.

I walk towards the Unemployment Centre and pass a lid on a rubbish bin we had photographed: 'Keep your hands out'. I smile.

The garden mirrors my personal growth – a discipline, just as writing this diary is a way of explaining the changes and allowing healing.

The letter written in response to our complaint to the National Health Service about your treatment is kindly veiled with the words that the treatment "we understood" you got was different to the one I and my daughter "thought you had received". They disagreed with my daughter's and my assessment of your care. We have sent one final letter to them and during an Emotional Freedom Technique visualisation I blew it away. Now I am going to draw a line under the whole episode.

I now patiently wait for the Coroner's and NHS reports.

Some of the autumn bulbs are already sending up little shoots from the dark earth.

I slept better last night, only waking a couple of times to go to the loo. I look at my watch, just as you did on waking, but then snuggle under the duvet and sleep. You often found it difficult to go back to sleep.

You felt at the end that we could no longer settle down together for the rest of our lives and make it work. Whenever you felt unwell it seemed a stage too far.

It was too difficult. You could no longer make the required effort. This became increasingly apparent. You would find somewhere for us to live. Invariably there would always be a reason why the place wasn't suitable. The tide was irretrievably going out.

Sweeping fear and anxiety would overwhelm you. You didn't want to be angry or friendless; you wanted to succeed but could not see a way. In the moments of hope you would embrace me gently and say it would work and we would overcome everything. Then your mind and body would be enveloped in an adrenaline rush where demons and confusion inhabited your world. Pages of indescribable torture, in a book about the holocaust that you were reading, became your reality.

You could no longer relax by the sea. Your mind was ravaged and elsewhere. You wanted it all to stop; everything to come to an end. Your mind was in a whirl. Some of it made sense but most of it was filled with a continuous bombardment of over-thought, nightmarish scenarios. This sometimes ended in attempted suicide.

You recognised the strain on me. I could no longer be pulled into this torment or be a bystander. Sometimes as you put it, I was your gaoler. You would invariably be sorry afterwards.

CHAPTER FIVE

I have my own home. The garden is where we are both free. I can nurture the plants.

I could no longer help or be responsible for you so we lived apart. Neither of us wanted to destroy the other. I could no longer cope. I did my best to explain to others how to help and give you advice. In the end we are all responsible for our own lives and outcomes.

You had become tired, very tired. On the occasions we met you were kind, loving and sometimes confused. In the separation there was no anger or bitterness, but the space to make decisions.

A coroner's court will decide what you finally did. You too sought rest, peace which this life could no longer provide. In that way we kept our love intact and allowed you to be healed, escape: and be safe.

I tidy the garden, pulling out the dead plants and cutting back the bushes. The time allows me to be grounded and bring a sense of order into my life.

It will soon be time for the clocks to change. This always seemed to affect your sleep pattern.

I see a small woodlouse in the downstairs shower room, pick it up with a piece of bathroom tissue and put it outside the kitchen window. You would do that with the tiniest creature or insect.

I go with your step-daughter to see the play Wife after Death, a comedy by Eric Chappell, who wrote Rising Damp, which you enjoyed.

You particularly liked Leonard Rossiter, who played the lead in tonight's play. It was a well-drawn farce, at times witty and sometimes predictable with a very ostentatious set.

You would have appreciated some of the puns and you would have picked up on the fluffed lines. The ashes get spilt several times, whilst yours are still in the bedroom in a green temporary plastic container. I need to wait until I know what people want do with them.

I pick out the returned marriage certificate, tear stained. I put it away. The marriage is still intact. We were living apart, but had not proceeded with any formal legal action. I decided on a two year separation before making any formal decision.

I am going to put a light in the burner, which reminds me of the candle I lit for you in church at Christmas. We know you were alive on 15th December and we will never know the exact date you died, probably the next day, 16th December. But officially it is 2nd January 2010. The date you were found.

I have bought winter pansies, which I can put in the front pots and transplant the fuchsias and lavender elsewhere. I was tempted to do it tonight but it was raining quite heavily and dark so I will do it tomorrow.

I awake from increasingly violent dreams.

I am carrying a glass container and having to go through a maze of construction. It is full of obstacles and in the process the container breaks. I go to fetch a replacement and in the end I am rushing so quickly, I bump into the ladder and cause untold injury.

I woke early in the morning and went back to sleep. Now, at 6.30 a.m., I get up and decide I will redo the pots in the back and front garden. I put new compost in them leaving only the purple-leafed violet untouched, and I replant them with pansies. They look neat and tidy.

People expected my grief to be contained. It has been nearly three months from hearing of your death.

I relight your candle in your burner eight times, and then let it be. Numbers were important to you, since your dad had played the treble number-plate game with you. This involved spotting car number-plates that had three successive numbers the same. These then took on a particular significance for you. Treble one signified being ill, treble

31

three was lucky, as was treble seven, treble nine not dreadful, but not good either, and treble four bad. I nearly got embroiled in your habit.

The bulbs that I bought in pots and replanted in the garden soon after your death are now in full bloom, yellow miniature daffodils and blue muscari and one blue hyacinth.

There was a daffodil in bud when you died and now it is bent over by the rain. The day before you died I had moved the driftwood pieces round the pots in the front garden to the back driftwood section. Before the policeman had knocked on the door I had attached a piece of black rope to the netting to the driftwood section of the back fence.

I know there will be good and bad days. I look at the head that I painted for the exhibition, half smiling and half crying, with flowered cheeks. It's alright to feel this way. I acknowledge our love and get on.

When my grandchild comes, it is funny listening to her breathing, softer and gentler than yours, and in the morning, wriggling, stretching and burbling songs, and refreshed from sleep.

You normally felt tired when you woke and could have tonic-clonic seizures making the whole bed shake like an earthquake. Your limbs were contracting and relaxing in turn. Your breathing was laboured and compromised. Sometimes you were incontinent or getting out of bed confused and disorientated looking for the loo and not always taking guidance. A nearby wastepaper basket was always useful to catch the urine. I'd guide you back to bed, where you would fall into a deep sonorous sleep.

My granddaughter is comfortable speaking on the mobile to her mum. You found phone calls difficult and the mobile and the computer a step too far. You did manage to do texts and taught me. You kept in touch with your friends in Canterbury until approximately 13th December.

I saw a friend who ran a local theatre we visited. She is producing The Importance of Being Earnest. I remember we took your mother to a production in Eastbourne at the Devonshire Park Theatre. She has now dedicated a seat for you in the auditorium. Joked to the administrator she hoped the view would not be obstructed.

Your night light is flickering and friends are coming to lunch. I must hoover. The orchids are blooming and the cowslip is re-potted and sitting on the back wall. Desert Island Discs is on the radio. This is one of your favourite programmes, and Waterloo Sunset is played, one you would definitely choose, whatever your mood or day.

CHAPTER SIX

Change happens. Habits can alter. Acceptance allows me to be in the present and then reflect.

Sometimes when I try to light it, your nightlight blows out. You disliked the shrine to your deceased sister on your mother's piano, now your pictures are there too.

I allow the hurt and anguish you inflicted on my children to disperse. I forgive myself, you and them. I allow a peace and a congruent resolution to settle, which your death has gifted.

The seedlings are growing. I deadhead the polyanthus and daffodils. The crocuses are dying but the new baby daffodils are growing. It's letting the hurt go, allowing the new to bud.

I am part of you still but, like the imprint that you get when folding paper with wet paint on one side, the mirror image is always slightly different. One print I liked a lot, when it was prised apart, was partly torn. There was no hole in the paper, but a layer came off like grazed skin. The part of my life with you has gone, but it will be reflected in my future.

Much later, when I had healing, you spoke to the healer and said "I should be happy" and you were glad that I was getting on with life. You also said, "I loved flowers and the garden. My perseverance had helped me."

You sometimes fell and hurt yourself with cuts when you had a seizure, like the time you were in the public loo and I could not be with you. It resulted in a cut under the eye.

Today a birthday beckons. I remember my first birthday with you. You hid my presents under the bed. Now your presents are in a bed of earth growing for all to see.

I look from the workroom window and I can see the candle flicker. Sometimes you could be socially welcoming and at other times that was hidden under a coat of brusqueness. There were moments of unexpected delight when you could be just as you wanted.

Your mind misfired because the connections were not earthed. I am or strive to be grounded, but could not ground the two of us.

I read a book to my granddaughter that I gave her when you were alive. Spontaneously tears fall and she kisses me trying to stop the sadness.

I remember, when you were not well, stitching objects onto material for your nephews. The colours and textures absorbed and distracted me. Doing allowed me to focus. The action of the thread going in and out of the material mimicked breathing in and out. A child gains comfort in repetition as cotton reels threaded one by one grow and take shape into a long necklace.

In an 'altered state' your confusion was often accompanied by the feeling that you had died. You would emerge from this state unexpectedly. You were tired, and felt like a dish-rag that had been rung out, but normal.

You liked Latin phrases like 'caveat emptor' (let the buyer beware), 'nil desperandum' (do not despair), 'mens rea' (guilty mind).

The herbs have been planted in pots outside the kitchen door and the mint that was cut right down is growing green and fresh. It's a gradual transformation as my grief changes.

I need to find a way of coping with people who do not know of your death, find a way of going through the 'I am now a widow' bit.

There are shifts in the grief. It's like digging one part of the garden and then the rest begs to be dug as well.

You had times when you enjoyed punning and thinking up jokes. Sometimes the ideas flowed and when you were on form I suggested perhaps you should do it as a career. In Edinburgh quite a lot of the stand-ups started their career later on in life. One I remember was an accountant for years and then became successful as a comedian. You said it was a step too far. Humour was to give pleasure to friends and family.

I collect a parcel, the same thing I was doing the last time I saw you. I vary the route home. I come home and there are letters to answer. I feel tired and rage creeps up on me. I cry, but gradually and determinedly sort it all out, as you did after seizures. Your body calmed by the seizure, you tidied your paperwork.

I pick the dead heads off the primulas.

I light the fire with plenty of paper and wood and it takes and roars. Your body was double bagged like the broken windows of the greenhouse, which had double black plastic bags over them to keep out the cold.

You liked algebraic puzzles. When you were unwell and I finished a 500 or 1000 piece jigsaw puzzle, I felt a sense of achievement. Sometimes I had to redo sections where pieces were forced together. You just saw it as a series of pieces. All I did was patch up your life, but like the black bag on the greenhouse it wasn't a long term solution.

The more I dead head the flowers, the more flowers form. In clearing your stuff, the more I uncover. I stack the boxes I cannot deal with and put them in the loft until I choose to cope with them.

I scatter your ashes with friends who could not come to the funeral, in my garden, our garden.

Then, in the evening when they have gone, I go to the park where you watched cricket and football and scatter more there. The next day I take the remaining ashes to a nearby garden where I remember you being very calm.

The day before your birthday I feel as though I am a tube of toothpaste being squeezed out to the very last drop. It is as though your hands are round my throat. I consciously keep breathing deeply and clear my chest and gradually the feeling subsides. You would have been 57 tomorrow. The tears fall as though a dam has broken and I let them tumble and do not hold them back. I remember times of stillness together and I know I will be fine on your birthday. I am.

We go to the same Italian restaurant where we celebrated your birthday and my daughter's last year. My granddaughter tucks into her food and says what fun it is. We come home laden. I put the Buddha my daughter bought me for an early birthday present in the porch, between two appliqué pieces of wood with a blue heart stone. One piece of wood was for you and one for me. You gave them to me for safe keeping. It is a peace token.

I transplanted the seedlings in the ground well before our holiday in America, and as luck has it, it rained. It was cooler. So I made sure they were well rooted and watered-in before I left, and they survived the fortnight I was away.

I think to myself:-

You have moved on and need to progress on the rest of your journey and make it on your own. I must distance your old self and your new self and make a loving distance between you and me. You are in another sphere. You want me to root in and be strong.

The seagull visits the garden, which reminds me of the distance between us, I visualise our echoed parting and cry. As the seagull takes off I feel healed.

CHAPTER SEVEN

The sea is where I find solace. Water is my favourite drink.

The sea is a place where I find peace. I love the rhythmic sound of the waves and the quietening of the breath. I am lulled by the mesmeric movement of the waves. My eyes are focused on the beach, picking out the treasures that I can use for my art.

There is a burst of delight when I spy pieces of driftwood, which are shaped and textured by the sea. I pounce on them as treasure. There is a sensuous quality in their colour and shape. They retain the smell of the sea and are patterned by the waves.

The rhythm of the tide has its small crescendos. Sometimes there is a full orchestral roll of an elongated wave, others break pianissimo. Today is calm as the tide ebbs. There is a soft breeze.

Pieces of driftwood that I prized but now find less attractive I give back to the sea in a ritual. I acknowledge the sea's gift and let the pieces go to be reshaped allowing their sea-change, relinquishing control.

On another day the sea is surging, and waves crash and foam on the shore. My feet planted in the shingle, the swell and stones batter my shins. One wave surprises me and I stumble into the spray, but right myself and stand firm. I breathe deeply and watch the waves.

Your mind is elsewhere, racing patterns whizz, lightning reactions to words, double-entendres. You are an unearthed plug, you fizzle, and sparks explode. You want to be switched off.

"Stop it!"

I've come here to find a lullaby for myself. A sliver of stillness is captured in the water's reflection. I picture you sitting calmly by the lake in Kilkenny. The photo I took on our holiday is fixed in my mind. There are no ripples to break the image.

When I was first separated by distance and then death, tears intermingled with the warming spray of a daily shower. Now I imagine standing in the sun being cleansed.

Water. Ponds where ducks, swans, coots swim. I remember the stream where I watched a rare water vole swim amazingly fast between the fronds of undergrowth.

Swimming slowly and steadily up and down the lanes of a pool, the constant repetition of movement soothes the mind.

There is the excitement of a child jumping into a puddle and Splosh! Splash! Splish! Splosh! Splash! This exercise is one of my qigong exercises which helps energise the body and is done by flexed springy knees. The arms move together forwards, fingers tips meeting and then falling back again, relaxed.

A glass of cool water refreshes me when I'm really thirsty. Water mixed with paint on wet paper spreads its hue like magic. Torrential rain punctuates the four o'clock heat of my childhood Sudan and re-awakens the shrivelled seeds. The dressing of the wells in Yorkshire is celebrated with mosaic patterns. The coloured petals become intricate designs.

Floods devastate, their waters, mixed with sewage, devour countryside and homes. Tears ravage the face and swell eyelids. You always supplied a hanky. Where is it now?

Glistening tarmac after rain, drooping flowers revived. I like the sound of rain splattering against the window. Water being splashed onto mosaics brings out their true colour. Pebbles on the beach dull when dry, sparkle when wet. Water transforms. Dehydration, especially in the elderly, causes confusion due to lack of oxygen to the brain.

My tears of grief acknowledge the pain and help me to move on. Slip is used to join hardened clay to fresh clay, it is made with clay dissolved in water mixed into a creamy paste. A hardened piece of clay needs to be scored with a sharp instrument in a criss-cross pattern and then the slip applied and the same done to the section it's going to join.

White horses foam the waves whipped up by the wind. A whole tsunami could devastate everything in an enormous rip curl.

I allow the water to replenish me.

Water cleans the brush that has covered a discarded tin with an undercoat of colour. A pattern of colour decorates the outside surface. The colour has varied, according to the wetness of the brush. Outlines develop. These are embellished by adding the same colour or different tones of the same hue. The discarded object is transformed. I am totally focused.

I regularly water the plants during the summer so the roots grow strong enough to survive. It becomes a daily ritual. I visit the garden and notice the slightest change during a prolonged period without rain. Weeds are pulled as they shoot, and the first buds from cut-down winter plants remind me that life endures. It is the habitual focus on nurturing the plants with water that nourishes them and me.

The water absorbed by the earth and then by plant roots is like my tears which spontaneously roll. It's a release, and healing. Grief and happiness are interconnected and as I let go of one so I can gradually accept the other. It is the fluidity of thought that lets this happen.

I go back to my source, our source, so we can move on. I create an intercellular vision, framing a picture in my mind. I remember the times when I was stressed. I fought you on the beach. I could not cope with looking after you, Pop, family, let alone myself. I go back to you as your future and ask your permission to change the scene. I do not want this trauma to haunt me. You accept me and we want to be healed and forgiven. I imagine us looking at a beautiful sunset together, holding hands.

This scene is painted in bright translucent colours, it is taken into my heart and into the individual cells and then blown away in a bright green field of thought. It becomes a powerful white shining light, where it transmogrifies.

I give you breath from my heart to fly free as a bird, and rejoice that your wings are spread wide.

Then I stretch my body and drink the water to replenish me.

CHAPTER EIGHT

Nature provides a healing space. Small changes in nature give me great joy.

The cowslips bloomed twice this year, once in the spring and now again in the autumn, reflecting rebirth. Was this a special phenomenon? Yellow is a healing colour. Your favourite flower was a primrose, a soft yellow.

Cowslips remind me of childhood, walks up the steep hill to my granny's, violets secreted under their leaves. It could be that since my granddaughter made magic in the garden with her wand that this has happened. I helped her make her magic wand and she enjoyed sticking on the sparkles and painting it.

I am trying to rebalance my life and let go of what I no longer need. I am changing. When deciduous trees die down there is a node giving us a sign that there is still a potential for growth.

To flourish it is necessary to be grounded. Feet planted on the earth. The feet are rooted into the ground. This allows the body to be stable and the mind to expand as the branches of the tree spread outwards, upwards, without toppling over.

If a plant's root system is fibrous and well spread it has a firm grip in the soil, and is more likely to survive. The same is true for me.

I find harmony and peace in the familiar ritual. Over time new plants are established and come into flower.

In the greenhouse, I plant seeds which I regularly water, and as they grow stronger they are transplanted outside. Their seed heads in turn will ensure that new plants will grow in situ.

Meticulously I dead-head flowers in the garden. Did you know it's very important to do that with rhododendrons, as when you pinch out the dead flower heads with forefinger and thumb, you allow new buds to form for the next year?

I take cuttings from established flowers such as fuchsia and lavender which will over-winter in the greenhouse and then, after the last frost, can be planted out into the garden. This mirrors the care I need to take of myself. With time I will be healed and be more resilient to your loss.

The garden reflects the journey we are both taking. You are leaving your concerns behind.

I decide I will paint the back wall. I buy tubs of acrylic paint, one white and two contrasting blue ones. They represent the sky which is limitless and the sea. I put some white on the warm coloured bricks and then experiment with shades of different blues. The blues are vibrant and I swish them on with a wet sponge with gay abandon. I try a couple of clouds, but cover them up. I splash white paint on the wall; swirling strokes signify movement and spray.

I was going to paint a sun but instead I hang my sun chime from a different part of the garden on the wall. The glinting red and orange of the chime contrasts well against the blues. I hang the driftwood bird flying upwards, and the holed stone heart I found on the beach the day after the policeman knocked on my door.

Above the wall is a bird table and from it dangle strings of holed shells and holed stones. I also hang a coconut wind chime which has carved birds hanging from it. The back wall has a ledge underneath it. I carefully rearrange driftwood, which I collected when I was still with you and after I was parted from you, into a small separate surround.

The ledge is interspersed with birds, different kinds of birds. One of which we bought together, the tiny metallic black bird, made out of recycled metal in Africa. There is a mother and a baby duck made out of bamboo and teak. A nodding mythical bird, whose body is carved out of wood, its feet and tail metal with a coiled wire neck. There is also a recycled wooden seagull made by locally unemployed people, and recently I have added a small scalloped metal bird bath with two birds sitting on it.

47

I made two birds out of clay and driftwood. I had put these on the driftwood section of my garden fence and both have gradually worn away. The driftwood fence is a conglomeration of driftwood, netting, and buoys. I re-remember that the day before I was informed of your death I had knotted a piece of black rope to this section.

When we were together in rented accommodation, I made a makeshift birdbath in a plant pot outside the sitting room window. It was a focal point. Once the birds had discovered the water we could watch them drink or bathe. First they tentatively sat on the edge and dipped their beaks in, staying initially for only a few seconds; there was something mesmerising in the way they swooped down. Others bathed and splashed and then ruffled their feathers, releasing the water. These moments gave us a sense of wonder. I experience an amazing feeling when I focus on seagulls floating in the sky.

In another part of the garden I uncoiled a thick rope and used the single threads to weave a net on a piece of driftwood, and I have woven in threads and shells into this white net. I have bought my sea treasures into my garden. Both my sitting room and bedroom have sea views.

One day I clear the dead needles from my two fir bushes. They had not been a priority. I also remove two dead branches. I spend time stripping the dead, brown, dried fir from the inside. I manage to remove most of it. It scratches my hand, but the smell of the pine is sweet and fresh.

I bag the debris into a double bag, as I know fir clippings discourage other growth. You were double bagged. Hopefully, like me, the firs will grow again. Now the light can penetrate and they will be encouraged to reconnect.

CHAPTER NINE

The garden continues to heal, as does spiritual healing.

I plant two sacks of daffodils, so that in the spring healing yellow will
be in the garden. When you died there was a lone daffodil in bud despite
it being bitterly cold. I have planted narcissi for their scent. I dig colour
into the earth. Their flowers will trumpet to the skies, where your spirit
flies, making me smile.

The roots will make them sturdy and stop further seepage of my grief.
No amount of plasters would have stopped your inevitable death. I root
myself and seal our love in butterfly wings, open wide against an azure
sky. It leaves a shimmering trail in my mind. A connection between two
distant spheres. You were always more interested in the night sky and
the galaxies than I was, and thought there was definitely life on other
planets.

I cut down the sunflowers and take the seeds out. Some I leave scattered
on the paved area for the birds. Others I spread into the sunken pond.
The rest I store in a Kilner jar to save as food for birds or for others to
plant in their gardens. The drooping and dying heads have been around
for a long time. Snails have been particularly attracted to the leaves and
stems, even the flower heads. I dig them up and scatter the excess earth
back on the flowerbeds.

I cut off and dig up the cornflower seed heads. The garden is transformed from being a blotched painting, where the colours had muddied. Now the calendulas shine bright orange and golden yellow. The colours of the primulas and nasturtiums are exposed to the light.

I decide that I will no longer be a regular attendee of the local epilepsy group. You had epilepsy but I am now responsible for myself and I tell them I will help when I feel like it. At the moment it is a constant reminder of the problems you had. You would have been proud of me taking responsibility for myself.

I take my granddaughter out into the garden before bedtime and she brings her little watering can. I had lost the shed key while tidying the garden and clearing the rubbish. As she waters, a piece of silver glints in the ground. It's the shed key.

Gradually I am unlocking the door and reconnecting my life.

I have an amazing healing session. This involves lying on a couch. I am asked to take three deep breaths and then breathe normally. My eyes shut and I see shapes and colours. In the beginning the colours are quite subtle, mainly yellows some oranges and a lot of swirling translucent mauve, violet and purple. Colours of the rainbow appear at the edge of my vision. An orange deepens to red, and then a really deep crimson turns to deep maroon that clears to a bright vibrant red.

For a moment there is a lot of bright white light. I have the sensation that this is the deepest form of healing I have ever experienced. The swirling shapes and colours momentarily take on solid forms, which are glimpsed and perhaps recognised subliminally. The most vivid image is the body of a baby, which is translucent. You can see the blood vessels. This perhaps represents the fact that now I am ready for change.

Briefly I see a figurehead, a devil in dirty maroon; colours become blurred, and then billow away in clouds that become pink. Perhaps the demons or fears I have had, and you had too, are dissipating. There is a character whose face changes, who could have been Pop, with whom I have a difficult emotional relationship.

The other very strong image is a coffin with a grey green silky covering which is slipping off. It then becomes a very white porcelain star. When the coffin appears I experience a sensation of coolness, but no fear. I mention this to the healer. He says he had felt the presence of a spirit who wanted to say sorry to my children. In the last few days I have felt that you have moved on and are feeling more at peace.

I choose to remember the good times and let go the bad. The dread and fear has gone.

My granddaughter wakes and sometimes screams that she is wet. Sometimes you wet the bed when nocturnal seizures gripped and relaxed your body, and left you incontinent. The unearthed fuse in your brain had let go of its excess electricity.

CHAPTER TEN

I continue to ground myself and darn my life.

My qigong exercises give me equilibrium. Each foot has three points of connection under the pad of the big toe, the little toe and in front of the heel pad. The triangle in-between the three points is called the bubbling well.

The garden is now more established and needs less care as autumn approaches.

A therapist works on my back and shoulders. Stress has caused accumulated tension over twenty-five years of care. She uses hot stones and Swedish massage which aids relaxation by deep heat. My body can gradually let go of the accumulated pain, as my mind releases anger and blame.

A friend gives me a perfect chestnut shell. I let it rest on my kitchen window sill. It has split and the shiny chestnut is being revealed. When curious hands split the spiky container too early, the milky white shiny coat has not yet transformed to gleaming brown.

My body has made a protective shell. In places it is still sometimes vulnerable, but a new person is emerging. There is a gradual transformation.

Living will always present challenges. I have a system in place whereby I tackle the problems as they arise and do not let them fester.

Gradually I am remaking connections with people I knew when we were together, making new friends, and filling the void. The repetitive actions used in my artwork, my continued tidying, adding new plants to the garden, and my daily routines, help to maintain a firm grounding.

The artwork is an unconscious link to me rethreading my life together. It reflects my core belief that the people on the edge of society need to be embraced and cherished.

I look up and see the crystal hanging from the hazel twig in my living space. The sun's rays have not yet caught it and splayed its spectrum. The magic wand sits safely in the same container. It is made of a discarded flag holder. A star made out of card with a heart is painted in vermillion and sprinkled with sequins.

In front of the hazel is an expensive cactus my daughter gave me for Mother's Day. It grows new spiky balls but over the years has never flowered.

I think of the writing class I lead and what new five minute challenge I can give them. The frog catches my eye, it's a wind-up toy; I will assemble several items in a bag and get the members of the class to choose three objects to interconnect together in a five minute exercise.

Friends want to meet. And they have suggested a place where you, I and the baby, my granddaughter, went when she was a few months old. It was a very happy time. You did not see much of her, but often she will help me light your spirit lamp on the back wall.

We visit the garden nearby where I scattered your ashes. She says, "Hello, Grandpa," and later, "We have to go now, goodbye. There's no need to worry!"

She has her box of toys at Granny's, her sandpit, her watering can and best of all she knows where the fridge is. As we get off the bus and we walk or push the buggy she says of Granny's house, "I've found it!"

The anniversary of the day we met, and the day twelve years later when we married, is tomorrow.

The conker shell on the window sill is opening. It reveals two perfect conkers lying side by side in a shell. In our separation that is what we can be. We are without pain and at peace.

CHAPTER ELEVEN

Routine is a comfort and cooking food is a joy.

My new-found routine gives me a sense of rhythm, of breathing in and out. This is underlined at the Steiner school my granddaughter attends. The routine is chat and tea, followed by a simple craft activity, tidying up and being outside in the garden, whatever the weather. We come in from the garden, hands are washed, bread kneaded, songs sung, and finally food shared and the 'Goodbye Song'. This is a time each week where I feel at home, embraced, like the children.

The preparation of a meal connects family and friends and it is a sharing and giving of love. Food is a necessity but also a joy in sharing its taste, colour, texture and presentation.

My maternal grandmother enjoyed cooking and was adept at making a meal quickly and efficiently. My mother enjoyed food, but not cooking. She'd prefer to take a pill with all the nutrients, rather than take the time and effort to cook.

When we were initially separated, cooking for myself only was a chore. I often filled the freezer with prepared meals that could be shared at a later date by others. I also find relaxation in cooking chutneys and pickles and seeing a row of neatly-filled jars. It gives me a sense of satisfaction and achievement.

I am very fond of my slow cooker. A lovely aroma fills the kitchen, and a stew can be prepared early in the morning and, on return in the evening, the meal's cooked. Cheaper cuts of meat can be used and the flavours have time to meld together.

I love soups which are thick and tasty and served with good bread. They are meals in themselves and can be followed by fruit or cheese. Nearer Christmas I like making sweets, which are fiddlier to make. Marzipan fruits involve repetition: putting in cloves as stalks, marking the surface with a kitchen grater to replicate the skin texture of oranges.

I can make pastry. I do not have cold dainty fingers. Normally I will use commercial pastry and roll it out. I prefer the act of kneading, amalgamating a mass of dough, turning it and pushing it in a rhythmical way. It uses muscle power; it's similar to working with clay, which I find therapeutic. What is more satisfying than eating freshly baked warm bread?

You enjoyed home-cooked food with friends. You felt more comfortable and relaxed eating at home. I also delighted in going out to eat, but you often found that the menus did not provide homely uncomplicated meals. Your palate and digestive system became upset by spicy foods, which I enjoyed.

Now I relish a good meal served to me. I choose something I wouldn't have bothered to cook at home.

I wake early on our anniversary and I put on the back wall a wooden dove we found when we were together, and a heart-shaped piece of chalk and a tiny wooden heart-shaped fragment. I light your spirit lamp, and I wish you peace and happiness on your journey and thank you for my freedom.

Today is cloudy, where yesterday was really balmy, the perfect condition for hang-gliding. I watch the open canopies floating in the thermals. It is a serene spectacle. A swatch of colour on the blue horizon, with a person perched on a bucket seat. One lands on the underpass where I'm walking by the sea. I appreciate the complex way it is threaded. If the threads tangled, how complicated it would be to sort them. However, when ordered, they enable the canopy to fly majestically. Perhaps my granddaughter when older will do this.

I find out that someone I knew briefly is terminally ill. She has been given weeks to live and wants no contact. As members of the group she belonged to for a brief period of time, we decide to send her a purple orchid. I find this out on our anniversary and it sends shivers down my spine.

I think of the healing that can be sent to her. She has her sons and partner with her. A feeling of a cocoon comes to my mind; I imagine her being in a bubble, no unwanted intrusion from the outside world.

She has control. A place where she can scribble and write where hopefully pain is managed as well as possible.

There is a distance, which is a preparation for separation from the familiar. I close my eyes and see a shimmering blue and a hazy sunlight. Blue is to cool the heat of the bowel, soothe the irritant mucus and constant peristalsis. I wish her a gentle sleep and rhythmical breath.

I send her stillness, an inner quiet, and thoughts to keep her grounded for as long as she needs them. I wish these thoughts to lift at the end of her life and for her to float freely caressed by a balmy day. The body feels light, no longer a heavy burden and is cradled, soothed in warm light and love. It is only a shell, which will open as conkers discard their armoured outside. Then their inner beauty is revealed in the silky wholeness, fear vanquished. The transformation allows the shrivelled husk to reveal its true essence, its splendour.

A friend who died momentarily between heart attack and resuscitation said he would not be afraid of death as he had experienced a tunnel of bright warm light which had removed any dread.

CHAPTER TWELVE

Intellect or instinct? Reality and truth were important to you and me.
When you were ill they became blurred. I'm instinctual, you were
analytical.

I have just been to see 'Certified Copy', a discursive film about the
authenticity of art and relationships. Do we call a forger who is
imitating an original an artist? Is the forger's work as precious or as
valuable as the initial artefact?

You always wanted to know about the artist, lyricist, writer, to enable
you to understand the work. You wanted to know the reasoning behind
the art. It made you able to appreciate it more. I am usually content
knowing I like something because it appeals to me.

I do remember being fascinated when we viewed the symbols
incorporated into various paintings of the old masters which were
explained to us when visiting a gallery in Amsterdam. This helped me
on an intellectual level, but did not make me like the painting more.
When I write, it comes from my mind, but also from a holistic
experience of finding ideas and words that produce a resonance.

Once a poem is on the page it is open to interpretation and others can
read it differently. The idea might have been specific to the creator
when the word order was made, or the piece of art constructed. People

bring their own meanings to it. Surely this is how art stays alive: it's being open to interpretation, which produces different views.

I do not despise the intellectual or technique. But I think of a dancer whose technique is faultless, but whose performance leaves me cold; and one who is able to express the emotion and with less proficient technique. I would always favour the flawed performance that had a dimension of warmth.

It is the element of being stirred by art, a book, dance, by that tenuous link that connects you with the artist. It is the engagement that allows the emotions to be captured. It is a thread of recognition, an undercurrent that weaves you into a moment of suspended disbelief.

While writing this I am using the little thesaurus you gave me one Christmas. I don't know where the big one went.

Perhaps it's because I am very tactile that the beach is where I feel caressed, now I no longer have your arms to embrace me.

Driftwood holds the memory of the sea. The sea has given the wood a new life. The constant movement of the waves breaks yet shapes it. Maybe the secret lies in the fact that I can rescue these fragments and make them into art. It gives me joy and nourishment and doesn't drain or deplete. They are like life remade. We too are making our lives again.

Does that mean I am a Buddhist? I don't really know. I know that you would remove the tiniest creature from the house and carefully put it outside where hopefully it would not come to harm. I am afraid I do not always have that attitude to them, especially to snails and slugs. Snails I tend to gather together and drop over the garden wall. According to Radio Four they will come back to my garden; they travel over thirty feet.

I have had an innate feeling that I have been 'here' before. There is a certain déjà vu when I visit places I have never visited before and they seem familiar. You also experienced déjà vu, probably due to your epilepsy rather than anything else. I am not sure whether we keep living our lives until we get them right. I believe that when we die we will be reconnected to those we loved. Sound waves do not disappear as our bodies do, and our souls will be reunited. The method does not concern me. It's an inner knowing. I do not have to understand how I breathe. It happens.

Do I accept this because it suits me or is it because it gives me comfort?

Your dread was that life went on ad infinitum. That really scared you. You thought at the end there would be an account book where all the good things and the bad things would be logged and accordingly you would either go to heaven or hell. You believed in a punishing God, a supernatural being. I tried to persuade you that this person was forgiving.

I am angry that your condition was never really managed or treated. I did what I could. When you were working things were better. You decided you could no longer work due to loss of memory, caused by seizures and prescribed medication. Your fear of making mistakes made you resign from your work as a solicitor. A vital work routine was lost and things quickly deteriorated.

I magic away the tears and look at the wand. Your mind is mended and you have found tranquillity, which so often evaded you 'here'. You did not like tears, so I stop crying.

I look at the conkers I found. They will be taken to the Steiner where they will each become the centre of a web pierced with cocktail sticks. The latter the children will wind round with white thread and the bottom of a teasel becomes the spider in the web.

CHAPTER THIRTEEN

Random connections like haphazard pickings from the beach link me back into life.

I am awake. I have now found a space where I can sell my artwork. The money raised can go towards the Whitehawk Inn. This is a centre for learning and support for the community. This place has also made me feel at home and given me a sense of purpose. The grief is present, but it fades away as I'm absorbed.

My granddaughter plays with her special board. It allows her to draw and then magically the picture disappears. We laugh and ask, "Where has it gone?"

My granddaughter makes a physical connection with her dad. She's seen him on Skype and talked occasionally. He was able to come and see her for a very brief visit. He was glad she had extended family nearby that helped in her upbringing. Her dad is a Muslim from the Sudan. Her great-grandfather, Pop, was able to practise his Arabic as he was in the Sudan during the war and later on in the sixties.

My granddaughter's dad was full of admiration for his daughter's beauty and thanked my own daughter for letting him see her. My grandchild continued with her normal routines and the brief visit went smoothly. We plan to visit her dad next year when he returns to Austria to continue his education.

He gave her wooden statues from his country and a map which hangs over her bed. A photograph of my daughter, granddaughter and her dad is at granny's house and mummy's.

My granddaughter has been an unexpected gift, as it was highly unlikely that my daughter would have a child. She knew she would be a single parent but continued the pregnancy. She has coped extremely well and worked hard. I am overjoyed at being a Granny. It's an amazing and rewarding experience.

I get up really early and go to the beach, not one of my usual beaches, to collect driftwood. I had collected there previously on the way to a friend's house, and on that occasion had found a haul of suitable driftwood. It had been a spontaneous thought and my anorak pockets were full of finds.

I have an amazing dream after I receive a thank-you from the writer in the group who was diagnosed as terminally ill.

I find myself on a bus. Why am I here? It is filled with lots of people who know each other. I am the stranger.

The bus driver stops somewhere familiar. I have to mount a large paving step, and then pay a deposit for a moving trolley for my grandchild. I am in a house full of warmth and colour, where there is a party atmosphere, and then there are two men in a bed. They are fully clothed. One of them is disabled; I don't know how I know, but I do. I walk down the stairs and find washing hanging to dry.

I open the wood-panelled door with a round brass handle etched with circles like the rings of a tree. I step out into unfamiliar territory. I have a panoramic view of a mountainous terrain in browns, reds and sandy colours dotted with the occasional white stone.

I awake thinking it is much later than it is. My dying friend has woken me, sending a text in the early hours of the morning.

I think about borrowed time as I drift in and out of consciousness. The picture of the majestic landscape, unlike anywhere I've been in reality, is framed in my mind. The mountains are steep and escarped to the valley. The scene is freshly painted, and there is a hint of a hidden river cut underneath the valley. I think of separation. It is all very surreal.

When my mother was dying she wanted to be outside the four walls of the bedroom that had become her prison. I dressed in a little black number and we took a train. We travelled in a Pullman with pristine white damask table clothes and candles, serving delectable food. The windows revealed lush countryside full of the promise of spring, the horse chestnuts with their candelabras of pink and white.

I had always taken my mother on car journeys, either to the sea or the Downs. On her final night I conjured up the necessary sounds, sights, smells and tastes. She was a child wrapped in a warm familiar story world. She fell asleep and the feeling of the dread, of night and darkness, was gone.

Today it is a Steiner school event for Michaelmas, welcoming autumn and saying goodbye to summer. It involves cleaning and planting in the garden and then singing autumnal songs and sharing homemade soup, bread and baked potatoes. There is a real sense of family and caring in the event.

My granddaughter and I have a very Steiner day at her best friend's house. We make felted balls by winding wool into a small nugget shape. We then add on thin layers of Merino wool around the nugget in different directions. Wetted with warm water and soap, they are rubbed between our hands until they ping. They take shape and feel quite solid.

We clear the garden and granny is in charge of collecting all the wiggly worms. There is a sense of satisfaction in seeing the area swept, dug and tidied.

Today I wake up when it is still dark and decide I will scavenge three beaches. There is not a lot of driftwood. The tide, like life, brings in different things at different times to the shore. I find a few pieces of driftwood, rather more oyster shells, some netting and a buoy. Thick and white plastic with loops at either end, I put it with the other buoys in my garden.

On the last beach nothing much at all. Then I spy a perfect star fish and a lobster pot. How could I have missed them? The bottom of the lobster pot is half broken and coiled with a thick, black rubber belt. I manage to uncoil the belt, but a piece of string holds the plastic grid in place.

It falls off as I mount the steps, dragging it to the car. I put it into the boot and keep the lid down, but it won't close. I drive home very slowly and carefully. The main frame of the lobster pot is blue, similar to the aquamarine exterior paint of my house.

I care for my granddaughter for the first few days of my daughter's short break. My granddaughter occasionally shows frustration when things are changed, like crying when the light is switched off; but once distracted, she calms down.

A friend visits and picks up the diaries that I wrote when you were unwell. I did not want to keep them but transformed them into an artist's book. It reduces me to tears. Pieces of driftwood decorate the outer edges of the book. By touching the book, my friend made me feel vulnerable, like you were when I wrote the notes.

Now I must distance myself. I do not run away from problems, and this week I have achieved some good things, but the 'to do' list seems to be growing.

My friend sees a bright star shining in the distance, but later it was not shining as brightly. She thinks it was you. Your memory is still part of me and, like my geological stone, magically lights up when held to the light.

I'm more tearful today as I've been looking after my granddaughter and sometimes, as you did, she has night terrors. Hers, unlike yours, are soon soothed and sound sleep is restored.

CHAPTER FOURTEEN

I prepare for the Coroner. I tie your part of the driftwood section with mine so we are together. I resolve to draw a line under the issues of your care. I can only do so much.

There will be some closure next week at the initial inquest.

I buy some hyacinths from the garden centre. They have been lying in the kitchen, waiting to be planted in a large pot a friend had promised but not delivered. I plant them in the front garden in existing pots instead. I love the fragrance of hyacinths.

When you were well your sense of smell was not good. When fragile, your sense of smell was acute, and even my perfume could make you feel nauseous.

Smell is so powerful.

Violets remind me of walking a winding lane up to Grandma's. Their flowers secreted under green leaves and their smell so sweet and gorgeous, the purple ones more pungent than their white cousins. Interspersed between them were primroses, their fragile yellow flowers crowned with soft green leaves.

The smell of a privet hedge is succulent. Grass cut after rain has that special fragrance. The first wafts of salt air when travelling towards the seaside as a child is so nostalgic. The sulphur of a striking match, tarmac being laid, are both acrid and yet appealing. The perfume of a fresh pine cone just fallen from the tree is earthy green.

Rosemary has a strong fragrance. It was something I could not use while you were around, as it affected your epilepsy. Lavender or jasmine were fine.

I get diverted from perfumes, as I make God's eyes with wooden skewers and wool.

There are four skewers which are centred so they have eight spokes. I wind the wool round the spokes three or four times to tie them together. At first the spokes slip out of order but the more times one completes the circle the more they stay in place.

It's like me trying to spin my life together. The start of the process is more complicated. Once a habitual rhythm is restored life tends to have its own kinetic energy.

The back and the front of this weaving are equally neat and the repetitive movement is like building up a framework, which keeps me stable.

I light your spirit light in the morning. It is still dark. Tomorrow will be the initial inquest. When I look back at it, the spirit lamp, metal and with patterned holes, seems larger and is burning brightly. I assure you that everything will be all right. In truth I am consoling myself.

Today our writer, who is dying, is meant to be coming for a lesson with her fellow writers.

I have written a piece which is neutral. It was on my 'to do' list for the debating dinner to propose two things that I would bring into parliament and two things that I would abolish.

In the past few days I have had momentary flash-backs, vivid memories of you, but they vanish, scudding away like clouds. The recent weather has swept the clouds away and the blue skies are full of hope.

I will file my statements and a copy of everything I need for tomorrow in a folder. I have a map to show us where the court is situated. All the information is safely collated, and I can read from my notes and disassociate myself as much as possible from the event. It is all there in front of me, I do not have to rely on my memory of our past tribulations. I have a copy of what I need to say.

My daughter and I are having hot stone massages as a treat after the hearing. We have two free seats for a comedy show that night. You would have appreciated that.

73

The passion fruit cuttings that I left standing in water in the greenhouse have not died. They were drooping due to the heat. They will survive. My granddaughter says, "Don't worry, it will be all right. It will be fine."

You found decisions difficult. In the end, life made the decision for you. Nobody will ever really know what happened. We have done our best. Wherever you are, you will know that.

On Sunday I attend the Argus award ceremony where The Whitehawk Inn wins Charity of the Year. We all celebrate the success.

I have had a compulsion to buy bulbs, and the last lot I couldn't resist were from the 99p shop: daffodils with orange centres, and narcissi and double daffodils. I plant them in the second raised terrace wherever I can find space between plants. It's the strong urge to look forward to the spring. By the back door are herbs, nearest to the kitchen, and the top sunken garden is our peace garden.

According to the Steiner tradition, in autumn the gnomes are polishing their underground crystals. Things are going back to ground and dying down into Mother Earth. Then the crystals in the snow and ice will come to the fore. They have brilliant patterns.

The orchids have flowered, their old stems are dying and new stems are growing. The circumstances of your death will be clarified, but the verdict will not be decided tomorrow, and my life goes on. It was important to you that I should live.

The 14th October brings some comfort. The coroner is kind, understanding and relaxed. He explains the format of the Coroner's Court. It has unearthed more of the investigations into your death. They will try and piece the information together that I was able to give them and find the missing links. They will ask further questions and the final inquest will be sometime next year.

Other letters found in your flat will be photocopied and be sent to me to analyse. The mood diary may help ascertain your state of mind. Hopefully, with the overdose, you may have fallen unconscious, or had a tonic-clonic seizure.

Your post mortem says your brain was normal, so too the heart and lungs. Only nominal hardening of the arteries was diagnosed.

Your step-daughter (my daughter) and I both agree to see the psychiatrist and discuss our further complaints. We will then draw a line under your death.

The act of writing is harder than practical physical activity. I steel myself to sit and write now before the first streaks of dawn light the sky.

I add a large grey green rope, which on its watery journey to the shore had picked up other threads and a glinting metallic fish, onto my driftwood fence. I tie it together from one end to the other. It amalgamates the section which was yours to the other section. Now they are inextricably linked.

You are part of my life. When this is all deliberated and disassociated from pain, there will be no more ripping, wrenching or tearing.

CHAPTER FIFTEEN

Rhythms of life alter the pattern of the days.

I happen to come across a performance of drumming and dancing in a church. Two Nigerians beat the drums with energetic zeal and the speed is amazing. They perform a warrior's dance and afterwards I join in a small routine. It is fast, furious and powerful. The momentary exercise makes me feel truly alive.

This pulse, resonance, is an echo of our being, and like an elastic band it breaks if continually overstretched, and perishes if not engaged enough. Is this why I am drawn to the sea? The whooshing of waves is the subtle drumbeat that stimulates and soothes.

Afterwards I attend a comedic lecture based on Uri Geller. It entertains. A member of the audience guesses a concealed playing card. Another finds a hidden object.

I go out in the garden. Some of the lower leaves of the calendula are going rotten, although the flowers are still vibrantly coloured. I pull them all out raging against the decay. I let the underneath planting have more space. Enough seeds will have dropped for them to grow next year. Soon a black plastic bag will be filled.

There is a smell of the sweetness of crushed flower heads and the dankness of autumn. I tidy some more and sweep the leaves. I fill the bird baths which have become slimy during the summer months.

There is washing to do and phone calls to be made. I shower to remove the dirt from the garden. I have cleared some of the clutter, which energises me, and also consumes the precious morning.

A friend tells me how she gives treatments on an intuitive level. She performs them as a dance. The necessary energy flows through her giving the strength she needs. The therapy then evolves. The time the person allows themselves on the couch is as important as the massage itself. In this world, where we rush around so much, it is important to be still and absorb the silence and be with ourselves.

My mind wanders to the treat I gave myself before the Epilepsy Research UK talks. The Indian restaurant I chose had the same material framed on the wall hangings that a writing friend had given me. Silken material in a purplish hue, covered with red leaved stems, encapsulated the rich colour of India.

On the entrance mat was a single white feather representing peace. My granddaughter calls white feathers angels or fairies. My maternal grandmother was a pacifist during the Second World War.

The plates in the restaurant matched my grandmother's every-day dinner set pattern. Was it coincidence or serendipity that made me feel comfortable here? I was the only early diner.

My daughter's work is affected by lack of staff, unsocial hours, tiredness and constant stress.

Gradually the pulled threads that constantly pucker her life are being sorted.

A determination to convert the flat so that my grandchild can have her own room will allow mother and daughter to have their own space. A rota which gives her regular hours will allow a rhythm in my daughter's and granddaughter's life.

Yesterday, before my daughter came home from her pressurised job, I cooked a roast chicken with parsnips and carrots found in her fridge. I saw a red cabbage and quickly thought of stewing it with onion, vinegar, brown sugar and apples, all of which were to hand in my daughter's kitchen. Leftover onions, peppers, a courgette were chopped and added to mixed herbs and a tin of tomatoes to make a sauce.

My hands naturally grab and chop the ingredients. Autumnal colours in the tomato base and the root vegetables. Food is a gift of love. It is warming and healthy. My granddaughter had her chicken in some gravy and got sticky hands.

It's a simple meal easily cooked. I prepare meals for myself, but it's better to share. We grow as we nurture ourselves and others.

I successfully arranged for a team to video a programme of Whitehawk Wordsmith's Anthology reading at The Three and Ten, a theatre above a pub. I relinquish control as I have enough to do. I am beginning to give up responsibility and am gradually re-patterning my life.

A eurhythmy class at the Steiner school is very exhilarating. Thoughts and feelings are combined, mirroring nature opening up and closing down, mimicking the ebb and flow of the sea, flowers budding and petals closing.

My body, which was quite cold earlier in the day, is now really warm. The teacher helps us to absorb the fundamentals of the dance and its repetitions while we watch, and then copying helps us to absorb the various elements. The dance allows a feeling of freedom, and ends with a peace chant.

My writing style is a stream of consciousness. Threads of thoughts, repeated strands, weave the words together. The echoed layers build a cocoon giving me protection so that my grief will lead to a transformation.

CHAPTER SIXTEEN

There is a parallel between a felted picture and rebuilding my life. I am learning to remember but disassociate memory from emotion.

Survival is the foundation of life.

It is the basic colour laid down on a cut-out piece of drying-up cloth. The first task is to make up a thickness of many strands of teased wool layered in different directions. This is then decorated with coloured strands of wool to make a picture, either abstract or representational.

A piece of net fabric is placed on top of the design. The piece that is being felted is sandwiched between two cloths. The net fabric is sprinkled with warm water and then washing up liquid. Hands press the picture so it is flattened with a continuous circular motion. The whole piece melds together and forms an image. It is a constant rhythmic movement. Then it is uncoiled and, as if pulling off a plaster, the newly formed felted material is pulled quickly from the bottom layer, rinsed and dried.

This process fills me with comfort. How often have we seen a child or baby have a comfort blanket or special toy? These in later life may transform into something else. A blue long-sleeved, straight to the hips, pleated, twenties style dress, with a boat collar became my lucky dress. I felt good when I wore it and invariably had an amazing time.

I allow myself to be disassociated from grief, but at the same time I do not shed the love I have felt.

Does this mean I obliterate the memories of the past? Not consciously, but I let them seep into the background like an early morning mist. The dawn haze is seen as dew drops. The heat of the day will disperse the film and bring different colours into view.

You wanted freedom. So do I, as I reshape my life. Then we can both enjoy independence. I am not holding you to account. Memories will float in and out like birds on the horizon.

I have to concentrate on being grounded and practical. Then in time I can let my body experience a feeling of lightness and floating free.

This reminds me of the kites being flown in Kensington Gardens when my children were small. The flyers were a group of wheelchair users. They relished the freedom of their swirling charges plunging and then miraculously ascending the heights.

You never knew when your epilepsy would strike. Mostly you were able to keep your fear at a safe distance. When the fear was present it consumed you and rationality disappeared. Things altered. They took on another appearance. Fear lurked in the mundane. Hunger enticed you to eat strawberries, but after eating a few these mystery fruits could be poisonous and kill. Your altered state had filled you with trepidation.

The mind out of control is open to its own destruction. It is encased in black where all the colours are absorbed and cannot be identified. No light can penetrate its depth.

I do not want to go there. I do not want to recall the hole where seemingly there was no escape. You found a way out and that's all that matters. I cannot and will not dwell on blackness. There was no magic wand to wish it all away. My granddaughter's wand is here.

I have someone coming to supper and divert myself. I take the pre-prepared soup out of the freezer to defrost. I combine left-over vegetables and a tin of flageolet beans into a casserole. I pre-cook the wholegrain rice. I discover when emptying the vegetables from the fridge that liquid has collected under the two containers, and mop it up. I get on with the day. I have to keep focused and I know what I can and cannot do if I am not to overstretch myself.

CHAPTER SEVENTEEN

Funerals, memories, mundane things.

I wake up early. Today I am going to a funeral with Pop, my Dad. I feel fine. It's for a person who lived into her late nineties and I am reading one of Pop's poems celebrating her famous musical teas.

Your funeral was arranged by my daughter – your step-daughter – and me. I think you would have appreciated the time and effort we put into it, to get it just right.

Well, you were the perfectionist.

The music played was, 'Stairway to Heaven', as people came in and we sang 'Imagine', which is the song you played as a request when you first met me at a singles club. You fancied my friend with the bedroom eyes, and when we went back to her home you discussed football and cricket with her son.

We lived together for twelve years and were married for thirteen. We spent a week in Liverpool. There we saw the white piano played in 'Imagine', and heard John Lennon's recorded voice.

Your exit music was 'Waterloo Sunset'. Your choice of discs would have varied from day to day according to your mood. 'Waterloo Sunset' was a consistent choice. This was the one you definitely said you wanted played at your funeral.

My daughter read a poem about birds finding their way home on their migration flight and battling bravely in the sky at dusk.

I read 'The Day Is Done' by Longfellow. I spoke about you truthfully and lovingly and your brother-in-law gave an honest summary of your life. I quoted your favourite piece from 'The Four Quartets':-

> 'Time present and time past
> Are both perhaps present in time future,
> And time future contained in time past.
> If all time is eternally present
> All time is unredeemable.'

I live in the now. I live in the moment. My granddaughter cuddles next to me on the settee and we sing songs, gesturing the actions. She giggles and laughs.

I have completed the felted Christmas decorations and added loops to them, made out of tiny pieces of discarded felt. You would have been pleased that I managed to use the left-over pieces. You hated waste. You steamed off unused postage stamps and used them again.

I shower and wash my hair, something I have been meaning to do for days. The shower water is not running away very well. I smile as I remove a plug of hair. It gets flushed down the loo.

I have tidied my desk and dining room table. They combine as one. I have found my ticket to the debating dinner and look out the bottle of wine I promised for the raffle. I have written my speech for the debate on acts of parliament.

I complete two letters. There is some kind of order again. Both my daughter and I tidy and clear when we are stressed and find it therapeutic.

At Pop's friend's funeral the vicar in his sermon mentioned the growth of the soul after the death of the body. A husk discarded and a seed that can then blossom into a beautiful flower. I thought wrongly that I wouldn't be tearful. The music of well-known hymns and psalms stirs unfathomed depths.

At the funeral I read Pop's poem clearly and slowly and get through it without faltering. I go home after a buffet lunch at the back of the church. Later I take Pop back to his flat. I also give a lift to a friend who said she'd walk but has had two glasses of wine. She is in her nineties too and unsteady on her feet.

CHAPTER EIGHTEEN

Doing something different makes me happy.

I go to my qigong class, which is based on breathing. I can definitely feel the stretches, my fasciae, the little muscles are working. I make sure I have enough money to give my friend, who I am going on holiday with in January.

I pass an art gallery. It's an international photographic gallery. The Brazilian work is black and white photos, which have been painstakingly coloured with oil paints. The portraits exude eeriness. The German pictures are reflected in water in a container underneath the slide show. They are set in the sixties and seventies; professional and clinical snapshots, at the delicatessen, a picnic, and high rise apartments. The American collection spans the fifties to seventies and explores conflict – the shots are an eclectic collection covering the gun culture, marlins being caught, beauty queens, Christmas.

The theatre show I want to see is sold out. People are smoking roll-ups outside. Smoking has never appealed to me. My cousin bribed me with a promise of forty pounds not to smoke or drink spirits before the age of twenty one. A glass of wine is fine. I can do without. Food and tasty snacks are more my thing, savoury rather than sweet. But given a box of chocolates, if I start on one, I would probably gobble the lot.

I stay in the hope that someone has a spare ticket, and they do. Quite often you and I would wait at sold-out shows in Edinburgh and always be rewarded with spare seats.

A friend has read the first few chapters of the book and said it had a definite rhythm to it. I want the reader to be swept along and then relax like the out breath in yoga.

The show had a very camp compere. I lost my ring, gold waves on silver, during one of the acts, but unlike my wedding ring it was retrieved. The ring for our wedding had been remade from my previous marriage ring. It was lost gardening or at the beach. I thought the ring was due another life.

But this waved ring that you bought me spontaneously one Christmas I treasure. When you came home the last time we saw each other, you noticed I was not wearing the wedding ring. I explained it was lost.

CHAPTER NINETEEN

I meet you unexpectedly on a bus as you come back to visit friends. I have been to the Sorting Office to collect a parcel. It's the same office where soon I will collect the papers from the Coroner's Office. Grief, like upset bulbs, is opened and resealed.

You came home after I had collected a Christmas parcel from the post office and coincidently we were on the same bus.

You made me promise that this, the last time I was to see you, I was to be still for you, even just for a minute. You massaged my shoulders. I did not touch you. I had to let you go. There was no more to give.

I did bustle around making sure you had food. Luckily I had a beef stew in the freezer, your favourite, which I defrosted. Some of which you ate and the rest I packed in containers for you to take with you. It was near Christmas so I gave you a present and my windproof jacket as you were shivery.

I dropped you off at a friend's. When asked how they felt you were that night, your friends thought you were in good humour.

I knew, however, you were not really functioning but were troubled. You gave me a Christmas present, and then took it back. I gave you some of my poems and illustrations. You wondered whether you should have come back to Brighton and be visiting friends. You wanted me to go to Tunisia for Christmas. I said I couldn't. I had to make the boundaries clear.

You grinned and waved when we said "Goodbye."

Tomorrow I will have to collect the papers that were found around you at the flat where you died. The packet is collected and it is like dug-up bulbs whose roots are exposed, their fragile tendrils no longer grounded. It feels like a dam has given way and tears fall, anger mixed with rage. Your age is wrong on the post mortem. Other things are inaccurate. I was too protective, but the so-called experts didn't know what to do. You were at the periphery of mental illness.

I know I must eat. I ring a friend; do some financial stuff that must be done. I shower, dress, ready for a debating dinner. I visit a museum and divert my mind with artefacts.

I visit a friend who knew both of us. Later I meet up with another friend who takes me to the dinner. The conversation is lively and my speech is voted most popular. I wanted fruit and vegetables to be sold without packaging and children to be taught basic cooking.

The next day I see my granddaughter for an hour or so while my daughter exercises. I eat at home, go to the beach and collect finds for my artwork. I doze in the sun and then make it down to a comedy club.

The comedian makes a joke of being delayed by a suicide on the line when he is in rush. I do not find this in bad taste. In the evening I make myself a snack and then early to bed, snuggled in a duvet with Radio Four.

I concentrate on getting the chores done. This takes time. The distraction is good and my hurt has re-sealed itself. I feel steadier again.

I knew you were dead when the policeman knocked on my door nearly a year ago. At first it was silence, followed by hysteria and then weeping.

CHAPTER TWENTY

Routines focus me. I must keep strong and look after myself.

I turn to my habitual routines to focus myself. I do not want to stray into territory which would engulf me in helplessness. I have left the Coroner's papers away from the house.

I concentrate on what exercise I can do with my writing group. I will get them to do an exercise on colour, how they would describe a chosen colour to someone who is blind.

You hated choices. So an innocent question about your favourite colour was confusing. Your answer would be, you did not want to choose one colour above another. They were all beautiful. Perhaps that came from your debating skills; you would be able to debate from both sides.

I put the pen away. Shades of pink fluff are in the grey sky. The day has dawned.

I go to my qigong class and my teacher likens breath to the waves rolling on the shore. They do not rush. There is a definite rhythm of coming in and going out. A circular action allows space between the inward and the outward breath. The momentum of the waves is ruled by the ocean and the moon. I feel an inner quiet whenever I visit the sea. Perhaps the breath subconsciously follows the rhythm of the sea.

I see gentians in a shop and buy three to form a clump. The gentians remind me of clear dry skies, the Alps and skiing. The blue is healing and special. Gentians and edelweiss grow together in my memory.

I sit by the beach and the grey and white clouds stretch before me amongst the patched blue. I've come to the sea again for respite. The sun glints on the sea's far horizon, the rest is dark and bobbly. An occasional sail arrests the eye and a seagull swoops into view. The waves washing the shore are greyish beige.

People babble at tables as I wait for my pumpkin and ginger soup. The sun peeps out from the clouds. It is soothing on my face. It restores my energy from a fretful night. My grandchild's mumblings, early waking, and then gradually falling back to sleep.

I laugh when someone at the café said that Chelsea was clinical but Spurs played with passion. You would have loved that, being a lifelong Spurs supporter. They went on to say the smaller the team the more enthusiastic the supporters, and those teams who win less frequently, like Spurs, are even more excited when their team wins.

It's difficult to deal with wet beds again. I did when you had tonic-clonic seizures at night. Now I have to deal with an accident with Pop, who has been incontinent in bed. He is too frail to sit outside the bed for any length of time, so I cover the wet patch with a towel and bed pad.

He stands up supported by a Zimmer frame and takes the opportunity to pee in a jug which I empty.

I take off the wet pyjamas and put on a clean pair and put the washing on. We employ carers, so I leave a note for the carer as there is only so much I can do.

I make it to the writing group having managed to read Pop a further chapter of his brother's memoirs, which gives us both something constructive to do. Pop's failing eyesight does not let him enjoy reading books. But he does occasionally listen to taped books and the radio.

An old acquaintance comes in late to our writing group, someone who is unaware of your death. Her appearance is spectral. Her face distorted. Perhaps this is the effect of steroids, together with plastic surgery. Her frame is tiny and covered in a black fitted winter coat. Her eyes are sometimes wide open and other times little slits. Her mouth is pumped full of collagen and painted with a bright lipstick. Her occasional interjections are hoarse and intelligent.

I dread talking to her, but do so. She is rightly embittered about the spending cuts. She is not shocked by your death. She concludes there will be many more.

She rolls a cigarette and slides outside into a taxi. Obviously unwell, her laced black gloves are the last image in my mind. She asks if I have her phone number. I have. I cannot reconnect at this time.

I get home and the hall stand, which is in the sitting room, startles me. It has been taken there, as the porch is being painted. The shadow of the stand with its coats looms above me and beside me.

I send the woman in the writing group strength but I cannot let the image haunt me.

I must remain focused. It's difficult, 'necromancy' echoes in my head, the art of revealing the future events by the dead. I choose life. I breathe. I want stability, to do my writing and art, to be creative.

CHAPTER TWENTY ONE

Upset. Finding things that will keep me rooted. Temporarily hating rain but knowing this phase will not last.

I look out of the window and seagulls are circling the windy air. They remind me of vultures who pick carcasses clean in the Sudan. Ugly birds that prevent disease from spreading from rotting flesh.

I think of the little wooden ark, which I bought for my granddaughter. She occasionally visited us in the last place you and I lived together. It was a friend's rented house by the sea. At other times I too went back to visit my daughter and Pop.

The best places to buy good things were charity shops, which I still frequent, and huge car boot sales where there were always plenty of bargains. I still use the blender which I bought for three pounds to puree fruit or make soups. My daughter and I went to one on August bank holiday and she got a lovely fitted woollen jacket for fifty pence. It is one of her favourite items of clothing.

I watch some of the fireworks from the window. It's a good viewing place as my house is high up. You loved the momentary colour splattering in the sky. We used to go to firework displays and walk the streets near us and see the exploding jewels. They mirrored your times of joy when Spurs won, or a job well done, or a meal at home with friends.

You would have been interested in a Radio Four programme discussing life, is it a comedy or a tragedy? There was an anagram containing 'funeral service' or something similar which turned into a Scottish saying that there was even fun in death, but, so often like you, I should have written it down. Now I have forgotten it.

Today I hate the sound of the rain splurging against the window. It is like the frustration of a fire which continually splutters but does not really catch light. It invades my space and makes me pull up the bed clothes and snuggle down. My mind races, my body sluggish and unwilling to move.

It's still only early November, but I get up trying to find a Christmas present I've already bought for my granddaughter and, in doing so, uncover other presents. I tend to buy when I see. I sort the presents into a carrier bag and decide I will wrap them on a night when I am listening to Radio Four.

I go outside. It is dustbin day and one of my planters by the front door has blown over and left muddy heaps on my doorstep. The hyacinths have shot white fragile roots and I tip the bulbs and roots back into their pot. I move the planters so they receive some protection from the wind.

I feel like an upset plant myself this morning. De-motivated and ungrounded, I tackle a few delayed telephone calls, guttering that needed to be cleared, and ask for a tax deduction certificate. I make a dental appointment and get the car booked in for an MOT. Is this how you felt when you were alone? I don't normally hate the rain but today I really resent it. I have to stay at my daughter's tonight.

I think of my granddaughter and there is a glimmer of an inward smile. She likes nothing better than puddles. I find her missing puzzle piece under the settee. The cat and fiddle jigsaw puzzle is one of her favourites. I put the missing piece in my handbag so I do not mislay it.

There is a discussion on Radio Four about poetry being the freest form of self-expression. Poetry is not something to use for a political speech, which is better expressed through rhetoric. The language of poetry challenges one's cognitive processes because of its precision. Poetry is one of my favourite ways of expressing myself.

My friend has just learned how to use an email and is thrilled with the experience, which is infectious. We are both hungry. She treats me to a roll from the corner shop.

She treats us, as she feels so excited.

The torrential rain,

Everything looks bleak.

Walking down the street,

Even anoraked, I get soaked.

The cold grey chill penetrates,

Drills lethargy into a body,

Which is normally happy to get on.

Spirit drowned in dullness

That eventually lifts, as the sun

Disperses the gloom.

The wind and wet together

Combine to drench and bedraggle.

Thoughts that would usually

Be caught and be ticked

Lie soggy and un-tackled,

A wet mess over an action page.

Today the rain is not so desolate, just patched into the day, and so I am able to have some times where my brain and body react quickly and get things done, which lifts my solemn mood and breaks through the stagnation.

CHAPTER TWENTY TWO

Minimise frustration. I love you at a distance. I survive.

Frustration at things not getting done by others throttles me. I put a stop to these thoughts and determine they will not lead to chaos. I do not let the waste worry me. Untouched nourishing meals that are left and gone off are chucked out. It goes against my core belief instilled in me by my grandmother of not wasting food.

When I was six I can remember my maternal grandmother was always able to prepare something out of very little if unexpected guests came.

I do so if my daughter and granddaughter need feeding; I look in the fridge and concoct something warming and tasty efficiently and quickly. Even if it's left-over vegetables cooked with a cheese sauce and bulked up with pasta. A quick tomato sauce made with tinned tomatoes, fried onions and garlic sloshed on top. All is baked in the oven and a little left over cheese sprinkled on top.

I have lunch at the Brighton Unemployment Family Project Centre and find laying on the table, amongst other leaflets, a pledge to reduce food waste, plan meals, portion control, keep it fresh, and love your leftovers. I feel a warm glow of satisfaction seeing my own convictions in print.

Tonight the moon hangs crescent-shaped, a warm yellow glow in the sky. Darkness was something I feared as a child, and crossing a dark corridor from a lit bedroom was scary. You found the dark a restful place and didn't like me switching on lights when it was gloomy. My Mother, towards the end of her life, dreaded the night and always hated stormy weather.

This morning there are swirling winds and rain again. Still, although I'm reluctant to leave the warmth of my bed, I feel more together. I remove two of the bargain books I bought yesterday at a closing down sale and find padded envelopes for them. I unearth birthday cards and put the presents ready for posting. The rest of the month is busy with fund-raising events. I get the presents off early so they do not lie forgotten at the last minute.

Yesterday I went out when it was dry, beach-combing. The wind whipped round and chilled despite my being wrapped up warm. My fingers went quite red with cold. You wore leather gloves in cold weather. I hardly ever wear gloves; perhaps I'll change my mind.

The wind and rain are affecting me. I'm being blown off direction, being buffeted. It is a force beyond my control. It's another force to deal with amidst everything else.

I am sitting in the car and it's pouring with rain. At least I loaded the car when it was windy, but not raining as well. That's something. It's so blustery outside I have decided to sit and write in the car rather than face the weather. I just hope tomorrow will be drier.

I think back to yesterday when the sky was stippled in places, as if by a dry paint brush. The rain falls in bursts and echoes in a crescendo of windswept individual droplets lashed together by the windscreen. It seems to be a continuous onslaught. It feeds the earth, making it sodden. The rain is lessening. I will venture out and get something to eat rather than sit and wait. Now it's pouring again. It's my qigong class soon and then I can set up my craft stall. The rain's respite was momentary.

I take down the wind chime with the birds and untangle some of the strings. Some are too messed up and I cut the strings, like I had cut you out of my life, in order that you could try to be independent. I have mended the chime. Some strings I've re-knotted. On others the string is missing, like you.

You didn't know the secret of life without me or with me, so you extricated yourself from this life altogether. You had tried many times before. It's sad but true. You did not want to live life without me. If I'd let you return, I would have drowned, the morass of your problems choking me. You always said I would survive, and I do.

CHAPTER TWENTY THREE

Accepting tears will come and go, mirroring letting go of things that no longer concern me.

I remember your laughter

Your cutting wit and the moments that

You were content being you, debating a point,

Watching a sunset, engrossed in backgammon,

Going for a walk, cheering the Scots on,

Spurs or Sussex at cricket.

Difficulties discarded, getting on with it.

The double edged coiled knife

Buried deep down,

Transformed into a green frond.

The fountain splashes sunlit

Water, my tears monosyllabic droplets

Cease when my granddaughter

Pops her head up in her bunk

Glides into Granny's open arms

And snuggles with her on the sofa

Weighting down my body.

Love remains unaltered by a verdict

Of suicide while the mental balance of

Your mind's disturbed.

Your day in court is over.

The truth dispassionately assessed.

You would smile that I managed

To express my opinion, had the last say,

I'm still the same.

My breast tingles with lost hurt.

The poppies are about to open

Their papery petals.

No written memorials on a bench

You abhorred them as macabre.

Celebrate life in bloom sitting by

The healing fountain, which uses

Spiritual and earth energy.

Last night in a monochrome dream

Faces appeared, from middle aged

To you as a child. Your mouth, grimaced,

Distorts inwardly and a smoky

Trail swirls in the ether.

My interpretation is, all pain is absolved.

Un-watered for three days

Plants wilt; drenched with water

Magically they revive. I meet

A friend we both knew, who runs

A local theatre above a pub,

We see the musical 'Spring Awakening',

Death and life are all around.

I sleep soundly.

It's time to end this page

And turn to another to

Make fresh marks.

I have even found a new way of living and making new marks on the page. Sometimes tears fall. Now re-united with my daughter and my granddaughter I find joy. I've found a different way to love. You do not have the burden of thought. Your laughter is echoed in a giggling grandchild, free to take a piece of completed puzzle and say it's disappeared. We play a game of hide and seek. You have gone but your imprint remains.

It is extinguished from the print of court papers or legal matters, or account books, but remains in fleeting remembrances of you that I embrace and let go.

I let go of the failures, foibles, and fears and let you enjoy your freedom. You are beyond my reach. My scribbling captures a thread that leaves a pattern of holes. I remember from embroidery, by pulling out threads, a neat row of holes remain. Meanwhile I weave my life with new colours; I acknowledge old patterns and experiment with new designs. I accept that tears release sorrow but also embrace the new.

It's like clay in my hand; I must not work it for too long as it tires, becomes brittle and breaks. I work subconsciously and my cocoon opens and shows me new ways to make my mark. Infinity scared you, and yet space enthralled you. Thank you, I wouldn't have been without you, but I couldn't look after you for any longer. I have learned to live again, and you learned to find an ending.

I make space to illuminate a facet of a rough-hewn diamond. Now I live each day as it comes, a new present to unwrap and discover.

I take the bus to Tunbridge Wells on an unexpected free day. On the way, I edit the work I've done so far. When I get off the bus there's a farmer's market, so I treat myself to a lamb burger. Later on I have a cool apple juice. I talk to the stall holder and buy a bottle and some chocolate covered cobnuts for Easter.

I peruse the art locally. There's an exhibition of John Piper's work. He worked with architect Basil Spence on designs for the University of Brighton and the windows of Coventry Cathedral. He designed tapestries for Chichester Cathedral and the stained glass for Lamberhurst. He was also very interested in nature and wild life.

Ambling through the town I buy myself a straw hat, two pieces of jewellery to go into my present drawer. One is a pretty variegated necklace, delicate in blues and greens. The other, a brooch which is an abstract shape with muted colours painted in mauves, yellows, greens, and one square of red. These are in geometric shapes and I picked it out as it was unusual. The latter I find at an antique fair.

I pop into an art gallery, where the art works are beyond my price range. I enjoy two brightly coloured acrylic paintings of a mountain landscape filled with different shaped houses. I am attracted to the immediacy of the style.

The other two things that tempt me are large pieces of glass, almost like geological stones that were shaded in layers of red, orange and yellow. There are stoneware containers covered with paintings of people, which are like canvasses. The clay has been covered with slip and then painted with glaze and even the underneath is glazed.

The colours are subtle and the gallery owner and I like the one in blues and browns and oranges.

I buy my grandchild a cardboard Easter egg. It is pure nostalgia. I remember having one as a child. I choose one decorated with stick-legged bunnies and Easter eggs.

I always have a yearning for cards, and buy two packs from charity shops.

I visit various shops to buy disposable table cloths for my party. Eventually I track down the 'Catering Company' in Camden Road, and purchase table cloths, together with candles and candleholders, and decorations to celebrate my birthday.

On my way there I visit the Trinity Arts Centre and see photos of Camden Road on show. It's an area they are re-developing and is crammed with quirky and individual shops. I spy another art gallery, which I visit. This is full of unusual gifts. I pick out a glass heart, which is full of mauves and pinks.

You and I went to Tunbridge Wells quite often looking for a prospective house. We saw Dara Ó Briain perform at the Assembly Rooms. While exploring the town I had moments of discomfort but I concentrated on my breathing and these passed. We had seen a house which was on the outskirts and a nearby lane led to the woods. It was only a twenty minute walk into town.

Also, you liked Tunbridge Wells because it had a lovely little cricket ground. Once we stayed in a bed and breakfast near woods when you stayed to watch the cricket. They fed badgers dog biscuits in the garden. Occasionally a fox would come for food but was scared by the badgers.

If I remember, even the library was open on a Sunday. At the time you were changing your anti-epileptic drugs and the new medication had made you feel nauseous and everything tasted like cardboard. The cricket, however, was a distraction.

I pass lots of posh clothes shops, but am not tempted. I have enough dresses at home to choose from for my birthday.

I arrive tired at the bus stop just as the homeward-bound bus is approaching. Later on I glance out of the window and spy a rabbit grazing in a field.

Tomorrow I am collecting for the Whitehawk Inn for the marathon. The day dawns and because the seafront roads are closed I have to go over the top of the hill. It means I take the route which we used to go home from after visiting your Mother's.

Inexplicably I begin to cry. This was a familiar route but I haven't used it for ages. I concentrate on my exhalations making them longer so I do not hyperventilate. I gain some control. I acknowledge the twenty five years we had together. It is as though the wound of grief has temporarily re-opened.

Running along with the Charity bucket for the Whitehawk Inn I recognise a few people who readily donate. Afterwards my legs ache, but I suffer no long term ill effects. Grief will well unexpectedly and it's also near the anniversary of your birthday. I forgive you and myself and dead-head the flowers before visiting a friend for the evening.

CHAPTER TWENTY FOUR

Delicious food, tasty treats.

I decide I deserve a treat. I visit the Thai restaurant. I am their first customer apart from people ordering takeaways. I order jasmine tea. It's refreshing and goes well with spicy food.

I order spare ribs marinated and then grilled, followed by a mixed seafood dish with exotic spices and Thai herbs. I end with coconut ice-cream. The meal is delicious. I enjoy every mouthful. There is no need to rush.

You found it difficult to eat a meal in a leisurely fashion, even if we were out. We were both quick eaters and so is my daughter. But this is a luxury and so I savour every mouthful. The stickiness of the spare ribs and their succulence is a pleasure. I enjoy the spiciness and different textures of the various sea foods, mussels, prawns, squid, and crispy fried fish with fragrant jasmine rice. The coconut ice cream has chunks of yellow and thin, pink threads in it. It is subtle and beautiful, and being well frozen, takes time and effort to eat.

It is as though the appreciation of the meal is the equivalent of my digesting some of the grief that I have been through. I feel satiated and complete.

The owner of the restaurant commented, "You've done well."

It was probably a comment that I had eaten everything or chosen well. To me this underlined the fact that my grief, which will naturally be present from time to time, is under control. I have constructed a dam, which restricts the outpourings of my grief.

CHAPTER TWENTY FIVE

Reflections, a year since your death. Pop is frail and dying. Do I believe there is life after death because the idea comforts me? Perhaps.

It's a year or more since your death. The daffodils that flowered so dauntlessly despite the snow in January are a month later this year. I have planted more daffodils, yellow and some orange ones, their heads will bring healing and colour to the garden. I planted a myriad of primulas so the slate-grey days would have colour. I planted some on my granddaughter's birthday.

I have tidied and gradually restructured the garden but not as manically as in the first year. The broken terracotta pot that was shedding layers was hauled out. Luckily a spare green plastic container housed the small hydrangea. Some shards of the terracotta were saved to put in pots for drainage and the broken vessel was taken to the tip where a worker dumped it into the hard-core bin.

The garden has gradually transformed and small leaves are appearing on the hydrangea and the little hedge leading from the second terrace to the third. The crocuses, yellow and purple, are bravely showing their heads. Some of the bushes are in bud and the hyacinth flowers are protected by strong green leaves.

I have treated myself to pottery classes and am building a vessel for the garden, which I will fill with blue glass at the bottom. This will become molten and cracked during the firing process. It's stoneware which will be impervious to frost unlike terracotta. I am making ornaments that can be hung in the garden or given to friends. I experiment with the various glazes. I have added a tall metal bird bath to the sunken garden which I discovered in a small shop.

I have redesigned the driftwood section and am taking the old wine bottle holders away and some of the driftwood which was a bit rotten. I've concentrated on the coloured bits of string and debris which have been woven into a textured shape. Like my grief it takes on a different form. Outbursts of grief are less frequent, and I am getting on with life.

The psychiatrist who dealt with your case told my daughter and me that he felt a failure because you eventually took your own life. The only thing I did was to give him a typed list of the things he could have perhaps done differently. My anger has dissipated, just as the snow has gone; for now at least.

I have given enough energy to the fight and must protect myself now. I am sure kernels of what my daughter and I said to the psychiatrist, face to face, will grow and imperceptibly change his attitude. Just as adding different plants to the garden increases the range of vegetation.

This year I hang my Christmas decorations from twigs. I celebrate with a real Christmas tree in a pot outside, which I and my granddaughter decorate with silver stars. She sticks sequins on the stars and we add coloured twigged purple and red balls.

I still go and collect driftwood, and the beach is always a solace. I am amassing a large collection and it will be made into decorative pieces for the festival. I will need a friend to help me with drilling the holes. I will use the different shapes and textures in building trees and sculptures which can be suspended on wire, interspersed with shells.

I still try and maintain the rhythm of the day with my emotional freedom technique and also my qigong. Now I am faced with another death, more natural, that of Pop, who is becoming increasingly frail, and is confined to the flat and mainly to bed. His birthday will be in a few days' time, he will be 94.

Just a few close friends, but the event has produced great anxiety and confusion for him. I made a card with felt stuck on so he can feel it. Abstract daffodils with their blooms still sheathed in green.

Ironically he does not believe in an afterlife, yet he attended church regularly until recently. He preferred the King James version of the Bible. He found the ritual of the church service comforting and beautiful.

I have always had an innate belief that death is a state of transition. I would like Pop to go peacefully in his sleep and not to linger in this half-life, which I'm sure he too finds frustrating. Dutifully I visit once or twice a day. His care needs are met by personal carers and, when not, I and my daughter provide the care.

As a family we all enjoy the theatre and so did Pop and you did too. Pop gave up theatre visits when his eyesight failed and his hearing deteriorated.

Last night I went to the theatre and saw 'The Master Class' based on the life of Maria Callas – her back story and the drive and determination she had to succeed, despite moments of anguish. We enjoyed the theatre, but I can still enjoy it on my own.

Tonight I am going to the debating society to hear a friend speak. You spoke there too, but towards the end getting up in public and speaking made you extremely anxious. You would shake and become pale and afterwards you would invariably have a nocturnal seizure. You felt frustrated that the words would not come out spontaneously and you found it an ordeal to express yourself. At school you had enjoyed the art of debating, and in the company of friends enjoyed discussing a point.

Pop, in the midst of his confusion, can also be totally lucid, which you could be as well. He will quote poetry verbatim that he learned at school and university.

I am not academic or intellectual but enjoy listening to Radio Four. I love the feel of shaping clay. I enjoy transferring feelings and textures onto the page.

Art for me is essentially therapeutic as, when I do it, the intellect is not involved. I am responding intuitively.

I took part of the diary I wrote when you were very disturbed. I tore it up because the words were too galling. I made it into a collage. I allowed the pages to dry. They became pages in an artist's book that I made. Disturbing thoughts transposed into sensory pages. I cut out headings from the newspaper and magazines which read as follows:

Metamorphosis *(mixed media)*
Shadows Windows of Light *(mixed media)*
New Beginnings *(torn-up notes reconstituted)*
Past Cut Up and Contained *(words torn up sequenced as this extract)*
Torn Faded Images *(faded copy of torn-up notes)*
Riding the Waves *(seaweed stuck on blue background)*
Petals and Leaf Patterns *(pressed leaves and flowers)*
Make Connections *(leaf patterns cut out and stuck)*
Beach Driftwood Binds Them Together *(driftwood binder)*

My grief is changing too.

Sorting my driftwood into sections by size, I discover a box of shells. I take out the intact shells, putting aside the holed ones for threading. I look at the sunken garden on the top terrace. There is a section with chalk and scattered shells at the top where I had scattered your ashes. Forget-me-not seedlings are growing in between. I edge the entire earthed section with whole shells and chalk, which reflects the white paint of the metal bird bath decorated with two birds.

It is the equivalent of drawing round a defined outline of our peace garden. I decide to string some driftwood with holes drilled through and alternate this with shells on a piece of wire which I found on the beach. It will be a sculpture which will swing in the air and the broken bits of wood and shells are in a coiled shape.

Stumps of wood will become the base of a tree. The trunk of the tree is made from spindly bits of wood found on the shore. Larger pieces of driftwood are drilled centrally to make the branches. In between are smaller blocks of wood to give room for the branches to splay out in different colours and textures. In using these pieces of broken wood they become whole.

I add more primulas to the periphery. I move the birds to the textured netted area. The duck and the duckling sit on the mosaic mirror with driftwood. The metal blackbird is high up on the fence and the dragonfly too. They are no longer by your spirit lamp.

Tears fall softly as I go to collect my son and his girlfriend from the station. I remember waiting for you at the station. My tears still. We walk in the rain. You hated rain and often your spirit lamp does not light under these conditions. Your spirit lamp wall has an added blue glass and metal flower made by a friend. I have transferred a lot of the wind chimes to the back wall.

I visit my ex-husband, my children's Dad, to celebrate his wife's birthday. I join in their banter and side with his wife that one slice of cake was enough. He has been diagnosed with diabetes which must be controlled by diet and eating low glycogenic food.

I give several neck massages ending with my ex, whose neck was virtually immobile. I use oil to try and lubricate the muscle. He says I have healing hands and, massaging him, I feel any residuary hurt I felt towards him dissipate. His neck muscles loosen.

Today I did a big clear out of the art in my room. I had done this before your death and after. Now it needed de-cluttering again. I took some artwork down to a local centre, which is having a fringe festival exhibition based on Past, Present and Future as my work covers these themes. They were made of recycled bits and incorporated driftwood from the past. Some of them had decorated figures, peg dolls, which previously I had sold separately. One artefact was a reconfigured lampshade whose inside was painted in browns like the earth. Plaits

119

dangled down from it like roots. The outside had multi-layers of painted ivy leaves, material, peg dolls, and more coloured plaits.

I also cleared all my paperwork and the downstairs cupboard and a collection of plastic bags. It gave me a feeling of achievement. There's more to do, but it's a start.

Pop lies confused in a hospital bed. He wants to hail a taxi to take him, myself and my daughter home. The world is doubly distorted through his macular degeneration; he can see things that are not there.

Yet when my daughter buys a paper and gives Pop a crossword clue 'a holder for a pistol', he immediately mentions his brother's name, who was an excellent shot, and says "Holster". We smile and reassure him and say he will be able to get out of hospital when he is better.

The clay container that I made at my pottery class had superficial cracks in certain places. Like grief it sometimes breaks through to the surface. The sand in Christchurch, New Zealand bubbles through geological faults and makes cracks in the ground. The glazes will hopefully harden the surface and if the container is cosseted and taken out of frosty conditions it will survive, as I do.

Maybe next time I'll make a smaller clay vessel; baby steps initially and then stride out.

CHAPTER TWENTY SIX

*Journeys allow me special scribbling time. The first journey describes
our separateness, the second Pop's love of Kent.*

TRAIN JOURNEY NUMBER ONE

Yours is a one way journey. I lit your spirit lamp this morning on the
back garden wall. I'm taking the train, not the car, as before you would
always have been my side, reminding me of directions. Now you are not
here. It's safer, not to say cheaper, this way. I get up ridiculously early,
as we always did, in order to miss the traffic.

Now I sit at the bus stop, writing this. I shed a few tears. It's the first
time I've made this journey without you. I have taken a large bag with
me stuffed with goodies for our friends, who text me frequently. They
did the same for you until the texts went unheeded and the policeman
knocked on my door.

I'm sorting what remains. My last task will be at the inquest, the date is
yet to be arranged. There I can speak of what I know; no-one can ever
be completely in another's mind.

The garden is coming on, over a year since I moved in. The sunflowers are blooming, the cornflowers fading, wild seeds scattered, and the first red nasturtiums straggle in and out of the ground of the drained pond, our peace garden. The cuttings in the greenhouse are growing strong and the baby spider plants your mother gave me thrive. A sapling I found at Sussex Square is growing.

The primulas have weathered in, planted when you first died. Green-leafed, the flowers are dormant until they colour the ground next spring. The plants that friends gave me have taken. They are nicotiana, a sweet smelling plant which is in flower, and the salvia, which has bloomed and is now in seed.

The bus comes into view. I wait at the stop with a mother, whose son went to the playgroup I ran at Whitehawk. Now I have completed the circle I live here too, in a house you visited several times that overlooks the sea. I am involved in raising money for the Whitehawk Inn, which is a charity for community learning, where together with my family I've found a sense of connection and friendship.

I arrive at the station. Police are helping a person who is having a seizure. They decline my offer of aid. You had seizures too.

I catch the train. The journey has begun. I open the Sunday paper, drink cool water from a bottle and munch an egg mayonnaise sandwich.

TRAIN JOURNEY NUMBER TWO

I see a bank of primrose blossoms from the railway replacement bus. I arrive at Lewes. I share the compartment with noisy young adults recovering from birthday party hangovers. The sea at Bexhill, Hastings rises from behind a hill. The youngsters alight.

There's a sense of freedom, a whole day away. I've given Pop breakfast. My duty is done.

Primroses spied amongst fallen trees, and the train goes onto Rye.

Sun glints through bird nests in bare branched trees.

Lambs, new born, nuzzle in the valleys. I am finding time away from Pop's confused brain. He sees tunnels and believes he is being transferred to another room.

We are now coming into the ancient town of Rye, a Cinque Port close to Pop's favourite county, Kent. There are more blossoms in Kent than Japan; Pop lived there too.

Arterial ways glint water, ditches and streams spill and spread into the green landscape. Nuggets of knowledge stand out, dark sedge patches against the spring grass.

A cloud covers the sun. Momentarily I am taken by the panic that occasionally grips Pop in the early morning. He feels stranded and alone. The sun is shining on the Kentish village of Appledore which reminds me of the fruit blossom that will appear later. I think of coxes, the apples and the cox, who steers the boat. Pop was a cox.

Swans are feeding on grass.

Ham Street reminds me of ham sandwich, which Pop wants but cannot chew. Two turtle doves sit on a white blossomed bush. Yellow celandine spreads over the wet grass. I remember an article in the Sunday paper about the brothers Dave and Ray Davies. Pop and his brother did not fight. They are both very different, Pop academic and his brother practical.

My ticket is clipped, "So they know I'm doing my job," says the conductor.

Then Ashford International, where I change for Canterbury West.

Old age has stripped Pop of his independence. He can manage short walks with the Zimmer frame under supervision to the hall and back, sit on the settee on a special pressure cushion. Pop opens his mouth wide, and swallows. His swallowing sometimes falters, so to help him his food is pureed and drinks thickened. Pop talks but his voice is hesitant and is soft. Visitors are welcome but tiring; Pop's comment is "I'll grin and bear it". So why do I bother to encourage them? But if I don't Pop is worried that they won't call.

The train arrives at Canterbury. Pop went to King's School, Canterbury as a boy.

I turn left out of the station, straight ahead through a small tunnel to the recreation ground, which I cross. I meet friends. My day has begun.

CHAPTER TWENTY SEVEN

Glimpses, random pictured thoughts.

The garden is dead-headed and tidied. Sodden primulas, hyacinths whose colour has drained, are removed. Shrivelled daffodil heads snapped off. The tulips are now coming into season, adding reds and purples to the garden. Our peace garden is full of primulas, grape-hyacinths, dwarf narcissi, forget-me-nots and shrubs. The fig has budding leaves and the redcurrant bushes too.

When I come in from the garden I turn to the birthday list at the end of the address book. Yours is crossed out and my tears well. I am determined to celebrate my new stitched life.

There are moments for tears like at 'The Life of Riley', an Alan Ayckbourn play that ends with a Pink Floyd song which reminds me of you. Neither the full moon nor the new moon fills me with trepidation. They often signified your being unwell.

On my last day on holiday in Fuerteventura, you appeared to me in a dream. I could touch you and see you in every tiny detail. You knelt on the carpet, reading a book. You wore your old carpet slippers and a red and blue stripy t-shirt.

Normally I visualise you as an inner voice, texture, shape, never your face. I have no photos of you displayed in my place. I carry you within me. There was a definite connection. Our hands brushed each other and then you went. I knew you were safe and untroubled. You were reassured and ready to move on. Tears fell softly and stilled.

You would have enjoyed the tap and beat of 'Stomp'. I shed a tear, but amazingly I have a hanky. You always had a handkerchief and gave me it to me at opportune moments.

Tonight I am seeing the ballet, an art form you could not really appreciate. You liked me to dance for you alone, when the curtains were closed against the wintry night. Now I am seeing the ballet for me.

I studied dance to strengthen my weak ankles. I was taught by a fierce retired Russian dancer and her daughter, who was forced into teaching as her body shape did not allow her to perform. This may have instilled the self-discipline that has remained within me. I used to wake you early to give you breakfast and your pills. Now I do the same for Pop.

The ballet is called LOL (Lots of Love), by Protein Dance, a contemporary ballet company. It portrays looking for love online; networking with tweets, Facebook, winks, pokes, and friends. The dancers' movements are shaped and inspired by previous audience research. Rhythm, speech, photo projection, music and video enhance the spectacle. It is acrobatic, subtle, energetic, poignant and funny. People's need for love was emphasised.

One of the women seeking a date wants someone to play Scrabble with her. You would have sympathised with that. You liked to play cards, chess, Mah-jongg, and backgammon. At those times you felt at your most relaxed and comfortable.

You found the web a place of deceit and paranoia. Emails were secret weapons that I sent, because you could not read them. The computer was an alien place. You did learn to use it, but without practice forgot and found it frustrating.

I haven't forgotten you. I have learned to lead my life and do my own thing. The fear of what might have happened has dissipated in your death.

I remember that Italian restaurant when 'Tambourine Man' came on. Tears ran down my face. The music had pin-pointed my grief. The last night of the proms, although I don't think I'm nationalistic, makes me cry. I am moved by my granddaughter singing, 'Twinkle twinkle little star' and Elgar's Nimrod which was played at my Mum's funeral.

Tears can sometimes be controlled. I sobbed my way through the dress rehearsal of your eulogy at the thanksgiving for your life; at the eulogy itself there was an occasional tremor but no tears, you hated tears. I

practised my emotional freedom technique and it allowed me to deliver
the words clearly.

WEDDING

I went to the festival of flowers at St. Margaret's
Church, Rottingdean. I should have guessed, above the
Kissing Gate wedding bells and garlands of cream and
    white roses;
Inside, anniversaries celebrated in floral designs,
    and parts of the
Wedding ceremony too. It brought back memories
    of our visit to
Liverpool, to Hope Street, where at one end, stood the
Solid brick Anglican Cathedral, at the other the
    Roman Catholic –
Metal, cement, rocket shaped, with modern rainbowed glass.
Both housed books, where innermost thoughts were revealed.
You were moved to tears at the words of a husband, Dad,
Who had abandoned his family, and explained his
    unfathomable sorrow,
At not knowing what had happened to them.
Today I wrote in the book that the display had been
    very beautiful,

Acknowledged you have died, but our distanced love

    is unaltered.

The garden which I cherish is yours to visit when you choose.

This life had not given you certainty, or lasting peace.

Happiness, visited intermittently, a dragonfly swooping

    with iridescent colour.

Your sense of humour had been a survival mechanism.

The last time we met, my wedding finger was ringless,

Lost while gardening or collecting driftwood.

    It had been remade

From one failed marriage to a plain gold ring,

    for ours. Marriage

Meant a lot to you, we were together over twenty five years,

Twelve living together and thirteen married, and separated for

The last year, until you were found dead. I wear the ring you

Bought me from a modern designer, which has gold waves

On silver. It's by the sea I find solace, search for

    bits of driftwood,

Holed shells, which I weave into art that makes my life whole.

The act of creating is an absolution, like the joy you had

At making people laugh, and the innocent beauty of my

Grandchild, who helps me to rediscover the world.

TO POP

Last night

I spoon food into Pop saying,

"Open wide."

I place the beaker in his hands

And say, "Drink please!"

I should feed him peace and sleep.

It's time to go.

Pop does not believe

In an afterlife but

Finds comfort in the ecclesiastical service.

I feel death is not an ending but a transformation.

This morning I thread the wire hooks

Of my sea sculptures with coloured

String from the beach, and tidy.

The poem I read to Pop has been reworked.

I wrote it on the bird baths,

The ones Pop tended everyday

When he was well.

I cleaned and filled them yesterday.

The poem was too literal,

Critical faculties are still alert,

Amidst confused ramblings.

Pop takes the poem to read

Eyes are dim and distant.

Pop admires the quality of the paper.

I kiss him goodbye, and say,

"I'll see you later Pop."

Tears are saved for the bus ride home.

THE ALMOND TREE

The almond tree

Nestles delicate pink blossoms,

Their fragile beauty

Enhanced by interspersed barren branches.

These tiny clusters

Can be whirled away

By wind and storm.

Pink, confetti-strewn

Grass is the only

Sign of their transient

Perfection.

Their loss foretells

Green leaves,

Yet to come.

CHAPTER TWENTY EIGHT

Thoughts of you. Some will make me cry, others are fine. Your birthday.

Gradually things are being sorted and so the garden is maturing and new shrubs are becoming robust.

There are still triggers for tears like when the radio played 'Live and Let Die'. Perhaps it was because you liked 007, Sean Connery in particular, reminding me of our trips to Edinburgh. I stopped the car as I was on the way home from collecting on the beach. I looked at the sky filled with purple pink clouds which I caught on camera.

A comedienne was exulting about Edinburgh: the effort she put in her two shows, which act as a show-case for her work and potentially grab the interest of others such as the BBC. In Edinburgh we saw lots of shows together, and although you often got quite excitable we could sit amongst the performers at the Pleasance and chat, eat and drink. The Pleasance was a favourite venue as there were numerous locations round the courtyard, which offered a variety of shows. As we always went when the Fringe started we were often given free tickets, to boost the audience numbers, especially if they were going to have a reviewer in; the shows might be excruciatingly bad but so often were surprisingly good. We would then recommend new shows to others. You were good at sorting out the next day's programme and I would check that we could get from venue to venue in time.

Edinburgh is a city where one can walk to most places. There were plenty of Italian restaurants where you could get your favourite bolognaise.

We always wanted to do a show together in Edinburgh at the Fringe. You decided it would definitely have a comedy scene. You always said a dark or difficult subject needed some laughter to get its point over. You wanted to see how it felt to do stand-up comedy. So you booked a five minute open mike slot in a venue when we got home. I encouraged you to practise your routine regularly so you became familiar with the material. I knew nerves often affect the memory but if you had been through the content countless times then hopefully you would feel more confident.

We arrived early and had a drink and chatted. The performer before you had the mike taken away from him by the audience. He was a professional stand-up who had three months off and this was his comeback! When the compere introduced you as the next act he asked the audience to be kind as it was your first time. You went on pale and sweaty but managed your jokes apart from stumbling over a couple of lines when you forgot the order. The audience didn't heckle and you got a few titters. You came off very relieved. At least they hadn't taken your mike away and apart from uncontrollably shaky hands, you had survived the experience.

The next comedian was a teacher who had been doing gigs several times a week for a couple of years; he was astounded at your bravery. He had started in a café with ten friends. You had done it at a venue for over a hundred amongst strangers. He went down well with the audience and did an encore and we gave him a lift back to the station. The other comedian was waiting to be paid and didn't even know whether he would have the fare back.

We devised a play which was performed by a local amateur group in our local fringe festival. It tackled the subject of epilepsy – you came up with the brilliant title of 'Fitting In'. However, because of the stigma against epilepsy then and now, we decided, against our principles, to advertise it as a romantic play with a twist, to attract more people. A lot of the audience members said they wouldn't have chosen to come if they knew it was about epilepsy but were glad they'd seen it. You were always upfront about your condition, but found it excruciating to watch the performances and chat afterwards. The feedback, especially from those who represented epilepsy charities, was favourable as giving an honest picture of the condition.

Your strength and resilience showed through in your sense of humour. Here are a few lines of banter from a comedy sketch between two fellow comedians and friends in 'Fitting In'.

Duncan	Do you ever think of those poor blokes having vasectomies?
James	They say everything begins with a small prick.
Duncan	Speak for yourself.
James	Let's remain mates.
Duncan	The whole point is, there's no need for rubbers.
James	Bet it still costs a packet.
Duncan	Yes, unfortunately now all we've got is the notional Health Service.
James	The waiting list's so long.
Duncan	You go off the idea.
James	And then she won't let you have it.
Duncan	So literally you are in no man's land.
James	What's it like at the start?
Duncan	The nurse comes round, takes one look, out comes the blade and everything shrinks. She deftly shaves and you daren't wince, or say anything inappropriate in case that's me done for.
James	In other words you can no longer stand up for yourself.
Duncan	The needle goes in and then its two pricks.
James	You mean two pricks for the price of one?

Duncan	They have to do both sides. The surgeon cuts, pulls, weaves his mystical knots.
James	So there's no more semen.
Duncan	They supply you with a couple of pots.
James	What for?
Duncan	They need two negative samples for the all-clear.
James	Do they sound a siren?
Duncan	Then you are shipped off to the waiting room, a cup of tea. The nurses grinning as they go past.
James	Your wife arrives saying "All done?"
Duncan	You nod and say you're a cut above the rest.
James	She laughs and drives you home.
Duncan	That's the best lift you'll get all week.

****

Making quirky art has always been a hobby. The pieces of art soon multiply.

I donated some of the art that I made when you were alive to CompARTment, in the local open market, to raise money for art activities. They were happy to make a link to Epilepsy Action on their web site.

The cover of 'Rethreading my Life' is my latest piece of artwork. I'm often inspired by donated or recycled articles. A friend gave me an enormous bag of beads. I sorted them into colours, just like you sorted after seizures, getting your life back into control. I then sewed them onto a coffee bean bag. I sewed on a hand-felted flower decorated with jewel-like beads to represent the thousand petals of the lotus flower opening. This reflects my continued involvement with yoga and meditation. I also wound coloured threads round my small driftwood finds. The whole piece resonates with the different textures and colour now present in my life.

It's as though the sticking plaster has stuck and I no longer really weep. Yes tears swell, but no longer fall as they did when you were alive and we were living separately.

Band Aid reminds me of Bruce Springsteen and going to his concert at Wembley before Live Aid. The colour, bustle, excitement, wide screens and the front of the crowd being sprayed with water, as it was a very hot day.

Today the garden is being dowsed with rain so I just top up the water on the greenhouse plants.

I wish you 'joy' without the adrenaline rush. The joy of the sight of my granddaughter, who magics the garden; or of hearing from her Mum that she went out into the garden with her fairy wings because they wouldn't fly indoors, stands to reason, and although she jumped as high as she could she repeatedly asks her Mum, "Why can't I fly?"

I REALLY WANT TO FLY

I really want to fly in the sky
I've got my fairy wings, and flap.
Nothing happens although I try.
I jump and flap and try some more
It seems I'm in a fearful trap,
I'm shaken to the core.
I turn to Mummy, "Why?
Why, oh why can't I fly?"
I'm trying hard to get off the ground
And then I begin to sigh.
She says, "Please baby don't cry!"
Mummy swings me round and round

And very soon we fall laughing to the ground.

We see the sky it's so very very far.

Now I'm off on my scooter

Down the hill I whizz

Yippee this is good fun,

Just like lemonade fizz.

Come on mum, run,

Catch me I'm good at this.

As you said, you were always 'Born to Run'. Hopefully you have found your 'Stairway to Heaven' and we will meet at 'Waterloo Sunset' and the world will be inspired to 'Imagine'.

I long to feel your hands in mine, just saying, "It's ok," but deep down I know you are safe and no harm can come to you. The siren of the ambulance doesn't fill me with dread any more.

I make play-dough for my granddaughter. It reminds me of making bread with my children and now my grandchild makes bread once a week when she's at school. It's the routine that helps keep me sane. I enjoy cooking. You preferred eating at home rather than eating out, unless it was eating at friends, or we were on holiday.

Now I treat myself to spicy meals and exotic food, which was not to your liking, and if you did eat it, it could upset your metabolism and invariably you would have a seizure. Coincidental? We'll never know.

Yesterday evening I enjoyed a small curry before freezing the rest for another day.

I notice in the free paper that Spurs have retrieved an awful situation to still be in with a chance and I think of your happiness. Your friend rings me to tell me that his daughter had got the A-levels to get into drama school – you would have been thrilled.

I am at the cricket to collect for Epilepsy Action. It was something that you had tried to initiate some years ago and now the charity has been allocated a set day. The match is a limited over game between Sussex and Surrey. The ground is full as Kevin Pietersen is playing, and it is James Kirtley's last match. It is a sunny day, which has also encouraged high attendance.

The last time I was at a game we sat together in the stand. Your eyes focussed on the cricket, mine on scribbling notes, or drawing or painting, or knitting. A day at the cricket was a day in the fresh air and you found it relaxing unless it was a crucial game for Sussex.

As I check on the collectors at the members' entrance I see a familiar figure in front. He had been a friend of yours for many years when he played a dirty trick on you. He had phoned a prospective employer where you had an interview advising them of your epilepsy. During the interview they bought up the subject of your epilepsy, telling you they had been pre-warned by him. You didn't get the job. There was a period of distance after that but you had made it up before your death. I do not particularly want to see him.

But he recognises me with my Epilepsy Action yellow jacket and proffers an apology. He knows of your death and blames himself for your downfall. I say little, but accept his small change. I cannot be angry, only sad. He looked bedraggled with his recycled waste carrier bag, missing teeth, thinning white hair and tanned face.

The day after I check on the garden and the bulbs that I planted: some of them have been unearthed by a storm. I take a trowel and resettle them in the earth, bedding them back, just as my emotions were stirred and would settle again. I have to get ready for my grandchild. I treat myself to a visit to the beach. Initially, the pickings are sparse, but I make myself go further and find, huddled together, three nuggets of beautiful driftwood.

Your birthday was on 13th April. You would have been fifty-eight. I go to Eastbourne, where you spent your last few weeks. I've taken a friend, with whom I used to work in a special school.

We have a coffee in a café where you and I had a drink on several occasions. We look through the shops in the centre by the station, and eat in the noodle bar in the Enterprise Centre.

We do the charity shops. I pick up an unusual dusty pink cotton dress for the Sussex Writers Awards, a pair of cotton pyjamas, white and blue, a necklace and some carpet rug wool strands in packets. These I can use on winter days to while away the time. My friend has found bargains for her grandchildren too.

We end up in the Bumper Book Shop, where, at brightly coloured oilskin table cloths, we are served with a gigantic teapot for two and freshly toasted tea cakes. My friend sees a 'Galaxies' poster on the wall. She has been searching for this poster for her eldest grandson. She is delighted, even more so as it is the last one and is taken off the wall and sold to her at a reduced price.

We wander back to the car and then I attend my writing class in the evening, where the extract of my diary is well received.

I feel good all day.

A few days later I visit a friend's flat, where she runs an artists' café. It's in Eastbourne too, and she is the friend whose course on 'Creative Joy' I attended. I'll attend her preview at the creative co-op market. I feel relaxed in Eastbourne, but at home in Brighton.

CHAPTER TWENTY NINE

My birthday, time to celebrate.

Yesterday I had a party to celebrate my new life, my different life. I was surrounded by old and new friends, people that knew us both and others who didn't. I set up the table and decorated the conference room before my writing class.

I left a few things for my daughter to do, cut the bread, brought the drink in, opened the jars and cheese. It was a hot day and some congregated inside and others chose to sit in the garden. I tried to talk to all the people at the party, but it's difficult.

I introduced people to other friends. Some had not seen my daughter for ages or my granddaughter. I was overwhelmed by the kindness of the Whitehawk Inn staff, who presented me with a beautiful purple orchid and two metal star candle holders. The orchid has not stopped flowering for more than a year. It's been nurtured, like me.

I had cut some flowers. The stocks smelled rich and sumptuous. The empty pots were surrounded by a box of beautiful vibrant blue pansies and a magnificent iridescent purple zinnia. These were planted in compost and watered as soon as I got home and the cut flowers put into vases.

The night lights and chocolates, scarf and jewellery were all put into a large bag.

The purple orchid was put into my front bay window, as my previous purple orchid had just stopped flowering. I also had an eco-voucher for a spa, and a beautiful delicately painted floral glass night light.

The candles for me are for remembrance. As I blew my candles out on my birthday cake, tears fell spontaneously. My daughter was by my side and her eyes welled too and my granddaughter came into my arms for a cuddle and my mood lifted.

My friend helped me cut the cake and distributed it amongst the guests. She made sure I was ok. The cakes and cupcakes were made by my daughter's half-sister. Towards the end of the party my granddaughter became tired and tetchy. My daughter took her home to meet friends. The Whitehawk Inn staff helped me clear away and I gave the surplus to a staff member who was having a barbecue. It had been a spontaneous idea. It helped me spin a web which will become my safety net.

Today, Good Friday, I look after my granddaughter and get shopping for Pop and cook him pureed meals which can be frozen. I'm given another zinnia which is bright pink and with the other plants will sparkle in the sun.

At my writing class we complete an exercise on how the sun makes us feel. As it is Easter we write about how we would choose to be reborn. The answers vary from a bird, a tiger, a unicorn, fear, a sorcerer, a high priest cat, a dolphin, an aristocratic cat, and (for myself) a tiny apple pip that grows into a seedling.

I'm reconnecting with the world. There will be bitter and sweet times but I'm moulding a life. A life where there are times that I can choose what I want to do. I'm sitting on Eastbourne beach writing this before I go to a fellow artist's preview. Time set aside just for me. When Easter is early it coincides with my daughter's birthday or yours. But this year it's late and my birthday is Easter Saturday.

It will be a time to look at things with fresh insight.

I eat tiger prawns at Periwinkles overlooking the pier. I remember the family and you going to the bar at the end of the pier. It was an evening of fun and laughter. Its little cupolas are shining bright in the sun. They are old fashioned and quaint. I'll just look and not revisit.

I walk back towards the venue and I see Marine Parade and then number 28. A bow fronted house, smaller than the ones either side. I did not cross the road. I want distance from where your life was ended.

Later I visit the healing beehive, a beehive which is made on a human scale in the shape of a section of honeycomb, which you enter by a hexagonal door.

The bees are born as minute eggs and then turn into miniscule grubs, which can be seen under a microscope. Royal jelly is squirted into them and then they are encased in a wax cell where they transform and emerge as a bee.

I am given little balls of pollen, like you see hanging from bees as they visit flowers. These balls gradually dissolve in the mouth. The beehive is very dark, not scary. The sound of the recorded bees is loud and I relax on a white fur rug. I am no longer fearful of seeing where you died. When I leave the beehive, I am given sweet runny honey which had been collected from the hive the day before. You liked thick set honey. The beekeepers, I discover, were friends of a friend of mine.

Today is my birthday and I will be spending it with my family. I light your spirit lamp before leaving the house. It is early, I am on my way to give Pop his breakfast. I drop off Easter chocolate to my friend. Pop is confused and trying to get out of bed. I manage to change him and give him breakfast and his medication.

Later we go to a restaurant: my daughter and her boyfriend, my son and his girlfriend and my granddaughter. We have a delicious meal, of fish soup, with mouth-watering confit of belly of pork on mustard mash and cabbage. The lemon posset is scrumptious, topped off with raspberry juice and fresh raspberries. On the way home I venture to go on my granddaughter's scooter. What grannies will do when they have had a glass of wine!

Pop has been given an Easter bouquet of flowers – hyacinths, daffs and freesias – and my daughter and I have a lovely bowl of hyacinths in moss. I collect the essentials from my kitchen for my son as he's just moved into a new flat; the saucepans I had bought for you, but they were never used.

My son has bought pastries from the French patisserie and these we share at my ex-husband's. I managed a small raspberry macaroon, chewy and sweet. The phone rings as Pop had rung the emergency button for Care-Link, I rushed round and reassured him. A carer was already there. His mind was in overdrive and he was seeing things, hallucinating.

My daughter's boyfriend stays the night and is up with Pop from three am. I have the morning off from giving him breakfast and find an enormous container standing by a skip, which I rescue. I fill it with compost and a kumquat tree. Today, with my acrylics, I paint the pot with bold leaves and oranges and pale flowers. As I paint I feel the merest hint of a hand on my bottom.

No-one was there.

Could it have been you? I had also received a beautiful standard lavender which I re-potted and put on the terrace amongst the herbs.

I'm off to meet a friend to go to the 'Garden and Home' exhibition at the Brighton Centre.

My daughter's boyfriend dreamed of me on a beach, asking him to give me the number fours. He explains they were on the back of my dress. You disliked the number four intensely, and 28, the number of the house where you died, is exactly 7 times 4. I planted a seedling from Pop's balcony in a pot and placed it on the top terrace of my garden. It will grow strong. I am getting stronger too.

My life no longer consists of waiting but is made up of taking opportunities as they are offered.

The garden is tidied and weeded and the dross is removed.

At the exhibition I buy spelt bread and an orchid which is preserved in resin. We listen to a question and answer session on gardens and watch a cookery demonstration.

The next day I visit Firle where I discover the glades that have been made since the last great storm. There are cherry glades, also crab apple, oriental silver and gold birch, weeping yews and bluebells; then the lost valley and the little dell with the summer house.

The church contains the marvellous stained glass window by John Piper whose exhibition I had seen in Tunbridge Wells. It's stunning, and the colours are even more vibrant as the sun streams through the window.

The window depicts ewes, musical instruments, grapes, pears, a tree, the moon, and the sun. It's an amazing spectacle.

I also met up with the woman who makes horses out of found wood from the forest and by the sea. The sense of movement and life is extraordinary. She too lost her husband around the time when you died. The making of the artefacts absorbed her and my artwork does the same for me.

I buy a porcelain bird on a metal rod, which is bird feeder, and a metal robin to put with my collection.

ALLOW TIME FOR . . . .

Allow time for

Tree watching, sculpted shapes that

Outline the horizon, wintered filigreed edges.

Clouds change formation, re-engage imagination

Childhood faces on the moon.

Linger in a bubble bath, tension

Unravels as bubbles burst like champagne.

Time for a meal savouring the texture

Explosion of taste in a palette of colour

Share friendship, laughter, and ideas.

Explore a museum caught up in another's

Reality, abstraction, capture a thought poem

Time to stroll look at rolling waves

Peruse the shore's jettisoned treasure.

Bargain browse in charity shops spying

Something unusual a perfect present

Listen to a discussion, drama on Radio Four

Playing with colour, camera clicks

At glimpsed opportunities. Mind, limbs respond

To music releasing stifled emotion

Gaze skywards at rainbows

Entranced in a book, intrigued by dramatic characters,

Time to fly a kite beyond everyday

Allow time to . . .

Sea-swelled tears rise in the morning,

Blurs vision and I head for the beach.

Seek solace in waves that soothe

My breath. Eyes scour for smoothed

Pieces of driftwood, which I transform

Into artefacts. Occasionally I unravel

Sea-string, the act of unpicking the

Turbulent mess, I relax, as yoga practice

Brings quiet to a busy mind, so clay

Allows fingers to mould shapes

That evolve naturally, or as now the

Act of scribbling, brings words on

A blank page and "I'm here".

CHAPTER THIRTY

Pop's death is allowing him to shed his cocoon.

Pop has let the clasp of life go. He is in a coma, limbo, waiting for the dazzling light. This will no longer blind his eyes. Pop's agitation stops as I brush his hair and whisper softly that there is nothing to fear. Pop's body accepts sleep and his shallow breathing becomes more normal, less gasping.

This life is just one of the many journeys and another existence will begin. The discarded husk allows the seed to fall.

I take the bus along the coast and go down the steps to a café where I enjoy a bacon sarnie and moist ginger cake. I saunter on the under cliff walk. I am accosted by a woman who clearly wants company. She strides purposefully. I say I need to take my time, "My Dad is dying." She reduces her pace and stays at my side.

I show her the church at the next village and Kipling's gardens too. It was here that Pop and you had a peaceful time on his birthday several years ago.

She leaves me determined to continue her walk. I go into a charity shop and buy a dress in charcoal, reds and blue. I look at the blue. I stare at the sea, blue, like Pop's eyes.

The sea is shimmering.

When I come back Pop's eyes are still able to blink. He is still stranded on the shore.

The hospice-trained district nurse administers another injection. Pop's body is cyanosed. I tell him it is time to go on his journey. I sit there and encourage him to venture into the next world. A journey he does not comprehend. He loved the rhythmical words of the service and the ritual but did not believe in the creed or in the afterlife. Perhaps it was Pop's logical and academic mind.

Pop, as always, wanted to be in control. Pop was sucking my energy dry; I wanted to give him the power to fly. To find a place where there is no need of a body which has turned in on itself.

We play Pop's favourite music and read peaceful prayers to him.

Then my daughter takes over and gives healing and does a meditation. Pop's breathing alters and, half asleep, I still hear his breaths as I hold his hand. Pop breaths out for what we thought was the last time; as in life, we kiss Pop goodbye. But he takes one more small breath, having the last word and making us laugh. In the end, death is peaceful, no gurgles like my mum.

We told my granddaughter that Pop has gone to visit the angels.

I have a dream where he is trying to make me whole again in this life. Pop, you've invaded my body and space. I feel angry beyond reason. A visit to the sea remedies the rage inside of me.

I have days of phone calls and retelling the story. Gradually and with the help of my daughter and son the funeral arrangements are finalised. There are fewer telephone messages when I come home. Letters and condolence cards arrive and are duly filed.

I sort out pictures of Pop and the family. This means I see ones of you that are hidden away, and tears fall. I leave the album with my daughter and later can look through the pictures without hurt.

Today I have tidied, unable to sleep well. I move all my writing and art work into my spare room. I have painted the recycled desk with flowers and leaves. It's signalling a new beginning, the table downstairs is ready for friends. I need to reconnect.

I have been carrying on with my writing and art, but now my home can be a different place. The established garden blooms naturally. Occasionally I tidy it.

IVY

I pull down the ivy which has
Surreptitiously climbed the walls
And trellises. The ivy reminds me
Of Van Gogh and you. It has a bitter
Dank smell and Van Gogh's
Grave was covered with it.
I fill the black sack with its
Leaves. It's like picking on
A scab, tears loosen from
My eyes. The Coroner's
Court has announced its verdict
The scar can heal untouched.
I make a note that the garden benches
Can do with another coat of
Preservative and put the rubbish out.

CHAPTER THIRTY ONE

Celebration of life.

The celebration of Pop's life has been carefully planned and will allow friends and family to be together at the final 'party'. We have all done our best to make it a memorable occasion. We choose the Whitehawk Inn as it is a relaxed and accommodating venue.

I'm on a bus journey. I feel calm, no responsibility, and I can scribble in my note book.

Two important lives have ended. The duty of care diminished. I accept there will be tearful moments.

Last night I listened to Mike Brierly, England's cricket captain, recalling the Ashes victory. He remembered how 'Beefy' Botham re-found his form. You always thought Brierly was England's best captain.

The thread from failure to success is infinitesimal. Failure is the way to success. Some people may think what we personally deem failure to be success and the reverse can also be true.

Do we measure someone's popularity by the number of people at their funeral? Do we measure a person by the lasting impact they had on our lives? Is death in old age and fragility more acceptable than suicide?

The memories of the dead still ignite unexpectedly. They make us smile and cry as in life. Consciously death is part of life as the seasons continually remind us. We embrace each new season letting the former go. We learn to treasure the day and live in the moment.

Eyes can be open to wonder. Ears alert to sound. Hands feel texture and gesticulate. Nostrils sense smells. The tongue tingles with different flavours. Time is so precious; each of us needs stillness to be at one with ourselves.

There are holes in life. Holes allow threads to be pulled through to form a safety net.

I sit on the beach and pick up the dredged shells, grey, silver, and some blackened. They glint invitingly in the sun. In the shade they are ash grey. I choose ones with holes through them so later on they can be threaded on wire and made into hangings.

The day for Pop's funeral comes. I have practised the eulogy for the past few days. I do the final practice before the limousine arrives.

The limousine will follow the hearse from his home. The funeral director walks in front of the hearse and a bus stops. Pop would have liked that.

We shed tears and then slowly make our way to the crematorium. The flowers on his coffin are white, blue, purple interspersed with an occasional yellow head. They are elegant, like Pop in his blazer, trousers, tie and yellow socks that he wears in his coffin.

We have to wait at the crematorium and my daughter and son help carry Pop in.

The funeral service that he planned goes well and the crematorium is packed. There's standing room only. At the celebration afterwards family and friends are able to reconnect. Pop would have loved that.

The weather is fine. The vicar Pop chose made us laugh, as Pop did. It is a fitting end to a life well lived.

The tears I shed for Pop are different to those for you. Time had eaten into Pop's body and like a snake it was time to loosen his skin. Pop's memories will linger but the pain is different than the grief I feel at your loss.

I send the last copies of the service sheets and eulogies out to family and friends. The lists in the files are checked and ticked and done.

Pop's loft is sorted; letters of administration and valuations are arranged by the children. There is no need for him to worry, his grandchildren have everything under control. Anxiety is banished by death and Pop lives on in echoed laughter.

Your bird-bath duties have been taken up by me and by Pop's great granddaughter.

BIRD BATHS

As promised the bird baths are
Cleared of sludge and grit.
Tall daffodils and little primroses
Rejoice and the roses bristle
With new leaves nearby.
Off-white Hellebores whose
Outer petals are tinged with pink
Cluster amidst the yellow crocuses,
Radiant suns, amongst the
Stately purple ones.
Dog violets abound,
Peeping through the garden fence.
In the grass-edged beds
The fading snowdrops
Still bloom.

CHAPTER THIRTY TWO

I allow artwork to happen organically. I send your medical notes to where they may help others. They are no longer my responsibility.

Pop's funeral is over, each took their own part. I make sure there's food for everyone, as I did for Pop. I also transport unwanted possessions to the tip and to the Unemployment Centre, where they can be appreciated and recycled. I take your clothes there and they are well received. One of your suits means a friend can go to a funeral and wedding in the proper attire. That would make you smile.

Things need to be finished. Ends need to be tidied. There is a sense of tiredness. I'm frayed at the edges. I'm sitting in the car. Traffic goes past in spurts. It disturbs the trees and sunshine outside. I know the unease will stop. It's only temporary.

The mourning will ease just as rain gives way to the sun. I have to adjust to a new routine, a new fingerprint on life.

The thunderous rush of traffic reminds me to take time. I must do things slowly. Let things unfurl as a flower emerges from a bud. There is still shape in the week, which will gradually take on another form.

I have arrived early for my treat. The luxury is a pottery class.

I do not like going to new places on my own. I leave in plenty of time and then do some writing in the car. When I arrive the other students are already there. After a quick introduction, different techniques are demonstrated and we are left to get on with our ideas.

I like to work organically and so, with some guidance from the potter, work with the shapes which appear from my finger and thumbs.

I also attempt the paper resist, which allows paper cut-outs to be sealed with slip. These are put on a hardened clay surface then painted with an oxide and dried again with a heat gun. The paper can then be removed, leaving the cut out image visible.

The sea gushes relentlessly. Spray hits the promenade. The wind blows white horses on the murky grey choppy water. The sea opens the lungs providing momentary relief from concern.

I look up from my scribbling and a patch of sea is caught in the sunlight. I have no wish to drown myself in the sea. I want my sharp edges to be soothed by the sea, like those precious pieces of sea glass. The sea glints wet slate grey.

There is a fine green line that sketches the horizon, circling into the distance. The sky is blue and clouded. Clouds are appliquéd onto the silky duck-egg blue, their edges highlighted by golden threads.

The clouds change their formation, animated by the breeze. The rush of the water swelling towards the shore on an inward tide waits expectantly before hitting the shore. It allows the breath to exhale retracting and taking in new energy before another wave curls onto the beach.

My being is stilled. But time is ticking away, I have to leave. How lucky that I too live so near the beach, how lucky that the sea-change can restore my equanimity. I come home and sort out poems. I unearth poems you sent me. The clouds outside are tinged pink and purple.

Tears overwhelm me. They last for minutes. Minutes where I want your arms to comfort me. I know it isn't possible. It wouldn't be possible. It shouldn't be possible.

Tears are dried.

I know I must go through your medical notes that you left to see if someone can benefit from them. They must have them. If not, I must shred or burn them. I do not want to repeatedly uncover them. They upset me.

In life there were occasions when I could alleviate your symptoms. In death there is nothing else I can do, and I – and you – are moving forward. The time has come to deal with this and leave space for other things.

I will keep the last poem you sent me. It tells me of your love and that you are giving me my freedom. Do any of us know what love is? You were troubled. I tried to help. I cared. I did love you. In the end it couldn't last. You gave me freedom and I must not waste it.

Your health notes were boxed in Pop's loft with some of my writing files. Your other notes were round the house. It was time to gather them all together. I had been given the name of a professor who might be able to use them. Your body had been too decomposed to use, as you had wanted, for medical research.

These records, which could not change the outcome, can perhaps help enlighten others who have similar problems.

The task is arduous. I try not to start reading them, but put them into some chronological order. Those that are duplicated I rip and double-bag. Some I burn to ashes.

I think I have despatched the lot, when I find yet more. I buy a big envelope, stuff them in and send them in the post. I put empty plastic folders back in the file. The laminated file which you took from the mental health centre I return in the post.

I do this anonymously as your notes will be anonymous.

It's getting rid of a burden I no longer need. It was part of me for so long. It seems strange to cut the umbilical cord. I first feel elated like after giving birth. Then I feel incredibly depressed. I know I have done the right thing.

The notes were a constant reminder of the past. What could have been, but wasn't. They encouraged picking at the scab and digging. It is better to let it heal naturally rather than self-harm.

You wouldn't have wanted that. They did no good sitting contained, dead like you. Now they will be looked at by fresh eyes who will judge their worth. I must wait for their comments. They have taken an onward journey. That's a positive step. You would be happy with the decision.

I was responsible. Now I have handed the responsibility to someone else. I must not dwell on this any longer. When you concentrated on your health, you thought it would make you well. It had the opposite effect.

I must divert myself. I have booked two holidays. Holidays for you were unpredictable and, like your health, could fluctuate like the weather. We managed but apprehension occasionally lurked in the pit of my stomach.

I find myself alone in the car after a nice chat and a cup of coffee with a friend.

I continue my journey, passing through areas where you and I looked at suitable places to live. I go through the outskirts of the town where you last worked. I went near the facilities, which we had explored together, leisure centres, clubs and libraries. I do not stop at any of them. It felt like a skirting, filmic acknowledgement.

I find myself making my way home and to a familiar beach. When driving I feel quite alone. The loneliness you felt towards the end of your life. The loneliness I could not mend.

The sunshine blazes on the beach and I gather the threads from coloured netting. I pull them apart and begin plaiting them together.

Earlier, I had noticed my keys glinting next to me. I thought I had put them in my handbag. I wander further down the beach and pick up more strands of colour.

I get to the car. My keys are not in the bag.

I automatically tap my collar bone and say I will find them. I remember where I had been sitting. There had been a Chinese group sitting there. Also there had been a bright scrap of yellow material and a discarded cola wrapper. I ask the Chinese group, who were packing up, if they had seen my keys. They look puzzled. I mimic rattling keys. Frantically I scrabble through the shingle. Nothing!

I sit still in the hot sun, knowing I still have a spare key to drive the car and spare keys to my home. I look to the left and see a piece of shiny metal glinting in the sun. My hand moves towards it and pulls. My keys came out in a bundle from under the pebbles.

I thank God. It is a miracle. The broken key that is still on the bundle had been the clue.

You were broken but now you are mended. I could not mend you but in your next life you will be whole. I put them in my bag.

I resolve I will make connections. I am naturally sociable. We are all alone but, like sorting your notes, I must sort my life.

I have decided what courses I will do next term. Each day should have a focus so that life will plait together like the strands of netting I find on the shore. These I put in a display hanging in my living room. It has crocheted circles from which are hung beach finds.

Yesterday I felt hollowed out and empty. Fields are left empty or fallow after several years of crops. More than twenty-five years of caring have come to an end. It's natural to have a reaction.

I still care for my daughter and granddaughter. She comes and we delight in each other's company.

I have arranged to see friends, as having the canvas of the day partly filled in makes life easier. The seagulls are screeching in the sky and are nagging me to get on.

I look through my address book and resolve to reweave the web. It's like restringing a necklace and choosing beads which will reflect and resonate in my new life.

The sound of the singing bowl hums like a new pulse.

I must bring this scribbling to an end.

I have sieved through the inquest into grief. It's time to move forward and not dig up death and disturb my wellbeing.

Your notes are in safe hands and will be well looked after.

I tried my best. Grief is acknowledged, accepted and allowed to heal.

POSTSCRIPT

It's been over four years since your death.

I thank you for the twenty five years we had together. I thank you for my freedom.

I am grateful that I have learned to live in the present and dig in my roots and make a life.

The garden is still a focus. Now it's not every day, apart from when I water seedlings or the potted sunflowers. But at least once a week I tidy, weed or add new plants. I do this in the early morning, my meditative time.

Every morning I still perform my physical exercises which combine qigong, yoga and some chanting ending with affirmations. This grounds me for the day. My days have developed a structure through my hobbies, looking after my grandchild and running voluntary groups, together with courses I do at the Whitehawk Inn and elsewhere. I have relearned to give myself treats and not feel guilty.

I have rethreaded my connections with old friends, restrung my necklace with new people and also found time to write. I play with creative ideas which absorb me and bring my life into the moment.

I accept that there will be unexpected moments of sadness. Recently 'Imagine' was played at a funeral of one of Pop's friends. It brought back memories of how we met at a singles club. You requested that song. It was played at your funeral and I quietly sung the words. I acknowledge my feelings to the friend, who stood next to me at the crematorium.

My family, friends, The Whitehawk Inn, and the creative process have helped me appreciate my life. I accept each new day as a present, unfolding it carefully and enjoying the process.

The more I live in the moment, the more harmony, peace and equanimity evolves and so happiness allows me to spread my arms wide. I embrace life.

These poems are about loss and bereavement, mine and others.

THE PARTING

Peacefully
The morning came.
Tucked safely
In slumber
Death slunk unaware;
Bedclothes unruffled from the night before
Snuggled round her.

NOT THE FUNGUS

"I can't believe it.
The fungus has me.
Not the fungus eating me?"
I knew I was ill
But did not suspect
The parasite tendrils
Branching through me
Spidery threads stretch out
Sapping my body.
"What do I fancy for tea?
Caviar and chilled champagne."
Later they operate,
"Let me die,"
I screech
"Let me die!
Stop the pain!"
Some days I fight
Other days I give in.
Insidiously I am attacked
And my defence weakens.
In my death
The parasite perishes
And I am at rest.

DEATH IS ONLY SLEEP

They left me without a shell –
Bags, tubes and no dignity.
The prospect of more operations
To shore up my spine
And gym shoes on my feet
So I shan't slip.
All I have is anger
Which I let rip
That's my explosion
Against the inner voice
Whose unheard scream
Asks for help as they
Crush my bones between
Plates of steel
And wrap me in an aluminium sheet.
I want to die in bed
At home with loved
Ones by my side.
You know – you do it!
Death is only sleep
I want to sleep.

"DOES GREAT GRANDMA HAVE A HEAVENLY NUMBER?"

With plastic red telephone –
Your prized Christmas present –
You perched on great grandma's bed
Spied her black bedside phone;
Discarded your own. As a special treat
She let you dial the numbers.
On your birthday a few days later
You dial through to great grandma,
Shout, "It's Buster!"
Later the number is unobtainable;
You simply ask,
"Does great grandma have a heavenly number?"

PATTY

The day before she
Had her dog put down,
Paid all the bills, left nothing
Undone, had the operation,
Anything that would stop the pain
And sickness. After in moments
Of brief consciousness said,
"I'm not still here am I?
I should have gone a long time ago!"
Only a chosen few to visit,
No other friends or relatives.
She did not want flowers
Or others to see her
Like this, but to be remembered as
Elegant, witty and strong.

NIGHT'S THE WORST

Night's the worst,
The four walls close in.
I dress up in a little
Black number for you.
I take you on a train journey,
One we would both begin.
We escape and feel the
Sleepers beneath our
Feet, drink sweet drink,
Eat delicious food,
See mountains capped
With snow and your
Breathing slows.
Morning breaks you
See the sun's rays and sit
In the chair.
Later the doctor comes
And hopes the injection will work,
Just before lunch
Three rasping breaths
Means no more dreaded nights.
The daffodils you arranged
Stand tall.

RICHARD

My mother told me you had died

In a car crash, survival would have meant

You would have been a vegetable.

I did not cry. You'd been so alive.

The first person I'd had a crush on.

My mother thought I was unmoved.

Later privately in my room tears fell.

You wanted us to be lovers.

You were probably twice my age,

You gave me expectation and

Anticipation. They'd discovered letters

That I had written from boarding school.

That's how they knew there was

Something between us. It's still

There just as fresh as the discarded

Snake skin in the shallow grave

That made me scream and rush out.

You hugged me and calmed me down.

You were a part-time archaeologist

In the Sudan and full-time teacher.

I, a schoolgirl, had acted Juliet

In Romeo and Juliet that summer

At the British Council. It was

A set book for the year.

Fluorescent beetles crept over me

While acting dead. They left blisters

Carefully pierced by Pop who soaked up the fluid

With blotting paper

Lest the liquid seep and make new blisters.

You lived in Hantoub across the Nile

From us, and I in Wad Medani.

Now you, my first love, have gone over

The river Lethe. Did they put coins on

Your eyes when you died, I wonder,

Or leave food and cooking vessels as in

Those shallow graves?

SUDDEN DEATH

Death felled
Without warning
Minds lashed numb
Too great a burden
To comprehend
Like the great tree strewn
After the hurricane.
No time to say goodbye
To hands which turned
Restoring resonant grain to
Its resplendent glory;
Stood sturdily against the
Sea's surging stronghold,
Not lain fast and buried deep
But spun unfathomed
Into another sphere.
Comforter
Where is your quick jovial wit?

HARRY

Harry is a strong sturdy boy,

He has his corner and his toys,

Harry is a special boy

Sometimes he switches off

And cannot hear; goes into

A dream world where there is no hurt

And Mummies don't die. Sometimes he

Wants to cry with rage but then he

Remembers eating pancakes with mummy

And that was fun. Harry misses her,

But in his heart she's happy he's

Carrying the line forward.

Ba-ba looks after him, as she did his

Mother and his Aunt Julia too.

Harry's no longer afraid of the dark,

He blows bubbles that live,

He is saving his ten pounds,

The most money he's ever had,

For Lego and sweets.

WE ALL HAVE TO MAKE THIS JOURNEY

We all have to make this journey.

What kind of journey?

A special journey.

Where do we go?

We are not sure

We will stay in the memory of those left behind.

Will we be on our own?

People have gone before.

People will go after.

What does it look like?

Perhaps like a sunset where all the colours meet

Fade into darkness and are reborn at sunrise

Who decides when the journey starts?

Each person has their own special time.

They are just the same, but different

No need for earthly bodies.

We can no longer touch them

But our thought waves reflect on life.

Water cradles, we cry at their leaving,

Their memories colour our lives

As sunsets and sunrises remind us

Each day is unique.

Their love is unchanged

As they start their new journey without fear and pain.